Energy Transfer

elevate science

MODULES

SAVVAS

LEARNING COMPANY

AUTHORS

You're an author!

As you write in this science book, your answers and personal discoveries will be recorded for you to keep, making this book unique to you. That is why you are one of the primary authors of this book.

✏️ **In the space below, print your name, school, town, and state. Then write a short autobiography that includes your interests and accomplishments.**

YOUR NAME ....

SCHOOL ....

TOWN, STATE ....

AUTOBIOGRAPHY ....

....

Your Photo

The cover photo shows a thermal image of a person on a bicycle with the heat of the muscles and the bicycle tires.

Front cover: Thermo image, Joseph Giacomin/ Getty Images; Back cover: Science Doodle, LHF Graphics/Shutterstock.

LEARNING COMPANY

ISBN-13: 978-1-418-29152-5
ISBN-10: 1-418-29152-8
5   20

Program Authors

ZIPPORAH MILLER, Ed.D.

Coordinator for K-12 Science Programs, Anne Arundel County Public Schools

Dr. Zipporah Miller currently serves as the Senior Manager for Organizational Learning with the Anne Arundel County Public School System. Prior to that she served as the K-12 Coordinator for science in Anne Arundel County. She conducts national training to science stakeholders on the Next Generation Science Standards. Dr. Miller also served as the Associate Executive Director for Professional Development Programs and conferences at the National Science Teachers Association (NSTA) and served as a reviewer during the development of Next Generation Science Standards. Dr. Miller holds a doctoral degree from the University of Maryland College Park, a master's degree in school administration and supervision from Bowie State University and a bachelor's degree from Chadron State College.

MICHAEL J. PADILLA, Ph.D.

Professor Emeritus, Eugene P. Moore School of Education, Clemson University, Clemson, South Carolina

Michael J. Padilla taught science in middle and secondary schools, has more than 30 years of experience educating middle-school science teachers, and served as one of the writers of the 1996 U.S. National Science Education Standards. In recent years Mike has focused on teaching science to English Language Learners. His extensive experience as Principal Investigator on numerous National Science Foundation and U.S. Department of Education grants resulted in more than $35 million in funding to improve science education. He served as president of the National Science Teachers Association, the world's largest science teaching organization, in 2005–6.

MICHAEL E. WYSESSION, Ph.D

Professor of Earth and Planetary Sciences, Washington University, St. Louis, Missouri

Author of more than 100 science and science education publications, Dr. Wysession was awarded the prestigious National Science Foundation Presidential Faculty Fellowship and Packard Foundation Fellowship for his research in geophysics, primarily focused on using seismic tomography to determine the forces driving plate tectonics. Dr. Wysession is also a leader in geoscience literacy and education; he is the chair of the Earth Science Literacy Initiative, the author of several popular video lectures on geology in the *Great Courses* series, and a lead writer of the *Next Generation Science Standards**.

REVIEWERS

Program Consultants

Carol Baker
Science Curriculum

Dr. Carol K. Baker is superintendent for Lyons Elementary K-8 School District in Lyons, Illinois. Prior to this, she was Director of Curriculum for Science and Music in Oak Lawn, Illinois. Before this she taught Physics and Earth Science for 18 years. In the recent past, Dr. Baker also wrote assessment questions for ACT (EXPLORE and PLAN), was elected president of the Illinois Science Teachers Association from 2011–2013, and served as a member of the Museum of Science and Industry (Chicago) advisory board. She is a writer of the Next Generation Science Standards. Dr. Baker received her B.S. in Physics and a science teaching certification. She completed her master's of Educational Administration (K-12) and earned her doctorate in Educational Leadership.

Jim Cummins
ELL

Dr. Cummins's research focuses on literacy development in multilingual schools and the role technology plays in learning across the curriculum. *Elevate Science* incorporates research-based principles for integrating language with the teaching of academic content based on Dr. Cummins's work.

Elfrieda Hiebert
Literacy

Dr. Hiebert, a former primary-school teacher, is President and CEO of TextProject, a non-profit aimed at providing open-access resources for instruction of beginning and struggling readers, She is also a research associate at the University of California Santa Cruz. Her research addresses how fluency, vocabulary, and knowledge can be fostered through appropriate texts, and her contributions have been recognized through awards such as the Oscar Causey Award for Outstanding Contributions to Reading Research (Literacy Research Association, 2015), Research to Practice award (American Educational Research Association, 2013), and the William S. Gray Citation of Merit Award for Outstanding Contributions to Reading Research (International Reading Association, 2008).

Content Reviewers

Alex Blom, Ph.D.
Associate Professor
Department Of Physical Sciences
Alverno College
Milwaukee, Wisconsin

Joy Branlund, Ph.D.
Department of Physical Science
Southwestern Illinois College
Granite City, Illinois

Judy Calhoun
Associate Professor
Physical Sciences
Alverno College
Milwaukee, Wisconsin

Stefan Debbert
Associate Professor of Chemistry
Lawrence University
Appleton, Wisconsin

Diane Doser
Professor
Department of Geological Sciences
University of Texas at El Paso
El Paso, Texas

Rick Duhrkopf, Ph.D.
Department of Biology
Baylor University
Waco, Texas

Jennifer Liang
University of Minnesota Duluth
Duluth, Minnesota

Heather Mernitz, Ph.D.
Associate Professor of Physical Sciences
Alverno College
Milwaukee, Wisconsin

Joseph McCullough, Ph.D.
Cabrillo College
Aptos, California

Katie M. Nemeth, Ph.D.
Assistant Professor
College of Science and Engineering
University of Minnesota Duluth
Duluth, Minnesota

Maik Pertermann
Department of Geology
Western Wyoming Community College
Rock Springs, Wyoming

Scott Rochette
Department of the Earth Sciences
The College at Brockport
 State University of New York
Brockport, New York

David Schuster
Washington University in St Louis
St. Louis, Missouri

Shannon Stevenson
Department of Biology
University of Minnesota Duluth
Duluth, Minnesota

Paul Stoddard, Ph.D.
Department of Geology and
 Environmental Geosciences
Northern Illinois University
DeKalb, Illinois

Nancy Taylor
American Public University
Charles Town, West Virginia

Teacher Reviewers

Jennifer Bennett, M.A.
Memorial Middle School
Tampa, Florida

Sonia Blackstone
Lake County Schools
Howey In the Hills, Florida

Teresa Bode
Roosevelt Elementary
Tampa, Florida

Tyler C. Britt, Ed.S.
Curriculum & Instructional
  Practice Coordinator
Raytown Quality Schools
Raytown, Missouri

A. Colleen Campos
Grandview High School
Aurora, Colorado

Ronald Davis
Riverview Elementary
Riverview, Florida

Coleen Doulk
Challenger School
Spring Hill, Florida

Mary D. Dube
Burnett Middle School
Seffner, Florida

Sandra Galpin
Adams Middle School
Tampa, Florida

Margaret Henry
Lebanon Junior High School
Lebanon, Ohio

Christina Hill
Beth Shields Middle School
Ruskin, Florida

Judy Johnis
Gorden Burnett Middle School
Seffner, Florida

Karen Y. Johnson
Beth Shields Middle School
Ruskin, Florida

Jane Kemp
Lockhart Elementary School
Tampa, Florida

Denise Kuhling
Adams Middle School
Tampa, Florida

Esther Leonard, M.Ed. and L.M.T.
Gifted and talented Implementation Specialist
San Antonio Independent School District
San Antonio, Texas

Kelly Maharaj
Challenger K–8 School of Science
  and Mathematics
Spring Hill, Florida

Kevin J. Maser, Ed.D.
H. Frank Carey Jr/Sr High School
Franklin Square, New York

Angie L. Matamoros, Ph.D.
ALM Science Consultant
Weston, Florida

Corey Mayle
Brogden Middle School
Durham, North Carolina

Keith McCarthy
George Washington Middle School
Wayne, New Jersey

Yolanda O. Peña
John F. Kennedy Junior High School
West Valley City, Utah

Kathleen M. Poe
Jacksonville Beach Elementary School
Jacksonville Beach, Florida

Wendy Rauld
Monroe Middle School
Tampa, Florida

Anne Rice
Woodland Middle School
Gurnee, Illinois

Bryna Selig
Gaithersburg Middle School
Gaithersburg, Maryland

Pat (Patricia) Shane, Ph.D.
STEM & ELA Education Consultant
Chapel Hill, North Carolina

Diana Shelton
Burnett Middle School
Seffner, Florida

Nakia Sturrup
Jennings Middle School
Seffner, Florida

Melissa Triebwasser
Walden Lake Elementary
Plant City, Florida

Michele Bubley Wiehagen
Science Coach
Miles Elementary School
Tampa, Florida

Pauline Wilcox
Instructional Science Coach
Fox Chapel Middle School
Spring Hill, Florida

Safety Reviewers

Douglas Mandt, M.S.
Science Education Consultant
Edgewood, Washington

Juliana Textley, Ph.D.
Author, NSTA books on school science safety
Adjunct Professor
Lesley University
Cambridge, Massachusetts

Go to SavvasRealize.com
to access your digital course.

▶ VIDEO
• Energy Engineer

👆 INTERACTIVITY
• Get the Ball Rolling • Understanding Machines • Levers • Force and Energy • Interpret Kinetic Energy Graphs • Racing for Kinetic Energy • Roller Coasters and Potential Energy • Prosthetics in Motion • Types of Energy • Forms of Energy • Energy Transformations • Take It to the Extreme

📱 VIRTUAL LAB
• Skate or Fly!

☑ ASSESSMENT

📖 eTEXT

HANDS-ON LABS

иConnect What Would Make a Card Jump?

иInvestigate
• What Work Is
• Mass, Velocity, and Kinetic Energy
• Energy, Magnetism, and Electricity
• Making a Flashlight Shine
• Law of Conservation of Energy

иDemonstrate
3, 2, 1... Liftoff!

TOPIC
2
Thermal Energy 50

The Essential Question What happens when heat flows from one object to another?

Quest KICKOFF Keep Hot Liquids Hot 52

иConnect Lab How Cold Is the Water? 53A

MS-PS3-3, MS-PS3-4, MS-PS3-5

▶ **VIDEO**
  • Firefighter

👆 **INTERACTIVITY**
  • Flow of Thermal Energy
  • A Rising Thermometer
  • Methods of Thermal Energy Transfer
  • Heat and Reheat
  • A Day at the Beach
  • Solar Oven Design
  • Matter and Thermal Energy Transfer

📱 **VIRTUAL LAB**
  • Choosing a Snack Food

✅ **ASSESSMENT**

📖 **eTEXT**

HANDS-ON LABS

иConnect How Cold Is the Water?

иInvestigate
  • Temperature and Thermal Energy
  • Visualizing Convection Currents
  • Comparing How Liquids Cool

иDemonstrate
Testing Thermal Conductivity

Elevate your thinking!

Elevate Science takes science to a whole new level and lets you take ownership of your learning. Explore science in the world around you. Investigate how things work. Think critically and solve problems! *Elevate Science* helps you think like a scientist, so you're ready for a world of discoveries.

Explore Your World

Explore real-life scenarios with engaging Quests that dig into science topics around the world. You can:

- Solve real-world problems
- Apply skills and knowledge
- Communicate solutions

Make Connections

Elevate Science connects science to other subjects and shows you how to better understand the world through:

- Mathematics
- Reading and Writing
- Literacy

Quest KICKOFF

What do you think is causing Pleasant Pond to turn green?

In 2016, algal blooms turned bodies of water green and slimy in Florida, Utah, California, and 17 other states. These blooms put people and ecosystems in danger. Scientists, such as limnologists, are working to predict and prevent future algal blooms. In this problem-based Quest activity, you will investigate an algal bloom at a lake and determine its cause. In labs and digital activities, you will apply what you learn in each lesson to help you gather evidence to solve the mystery. With enough evidence, you will be able to identify what you believe is the cause of the algal bloom and present a solution in the Findings activity.

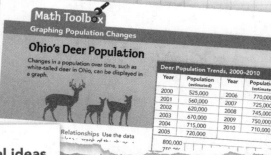

Math Toolbox

Graphing Population Changes

Ohio's Deer Population

Changes in a population over time, such as white-tailed deer in Ohio, can be displayed in a graph.

Deer Population Trends, 2000-2010

Year	Population (estimated)	Year	Population (estimated)
2000	525,000	2006	770,000
2001	560,000	2007	725,000
2002	620,000	2008	745,000
2003	670,000	2009	750,000
2004	715,000	2010	710,000
2005	720,000		

Relationships Use the data

800,000
750,000

READING CHECK Determine Central ideas

What adaptations might the giraffe have that help it survive in its environment?

Academic Vocabulary

Relate the term *decomposer* to the verb *compose*. What does it mean to compose something?

Build Skills for the Future

- Master the Engineering Design Process
- Apply critical thinking and analytical skills
- Learn about STEM careers

Focus on Inquiry

Case studies put you in the shoes of a scientist to solve real-world mysteries using real data. You will be able to:

- Analyze Data
- Test a hypothesis
- Solve the Case

Case Study

MS-LS2-1

THE CASE OF THE DISAPPEARING

Cerulean Warbler

The cerulean warbler is a small, migratory songbird named for its blue color. Cerulean warblers breed in eastern North America during the spring and summer. The warblers spend the winter months in the Andes Mountains of Colombia, Venezuela, Ecuador, and Peru in northern part of South America.

Enter the Lab

Hands-on experiments and virtual labs help you test ideas and show what you know in performance-based assessments. Scaffolded labs include:

- STEM Labs
- Design Your Own
- Open-ended Labs

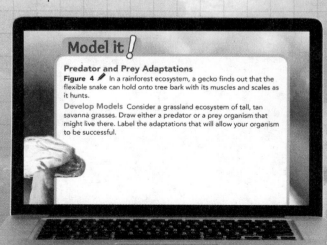

HANDS-ON LAB

uInvestigate Observe how once-living matter is broken down into smaller components in the process of decomposition.

TOPIC
1

Energy

NGSS PERFORMANCE EXPECTATIONS

MS-PS3-1 Construct and interpret graphical displays of data to describe the relationships of kinetic energy to the mass of an object and to the speed of an object.

MS-PS3-2 Develop a model to describe that when the arrangement of objects interacting at a distance changes, different amounts of potential energy are stored in the system.

MS-PS3-5 Construct, use, and present arguments to support the claim that when the kinetic energy of an object changes, energy is transferred to or from the object.

HANDS-ON LAB

uConnect Explore how changes in energy can make a playing card jump.

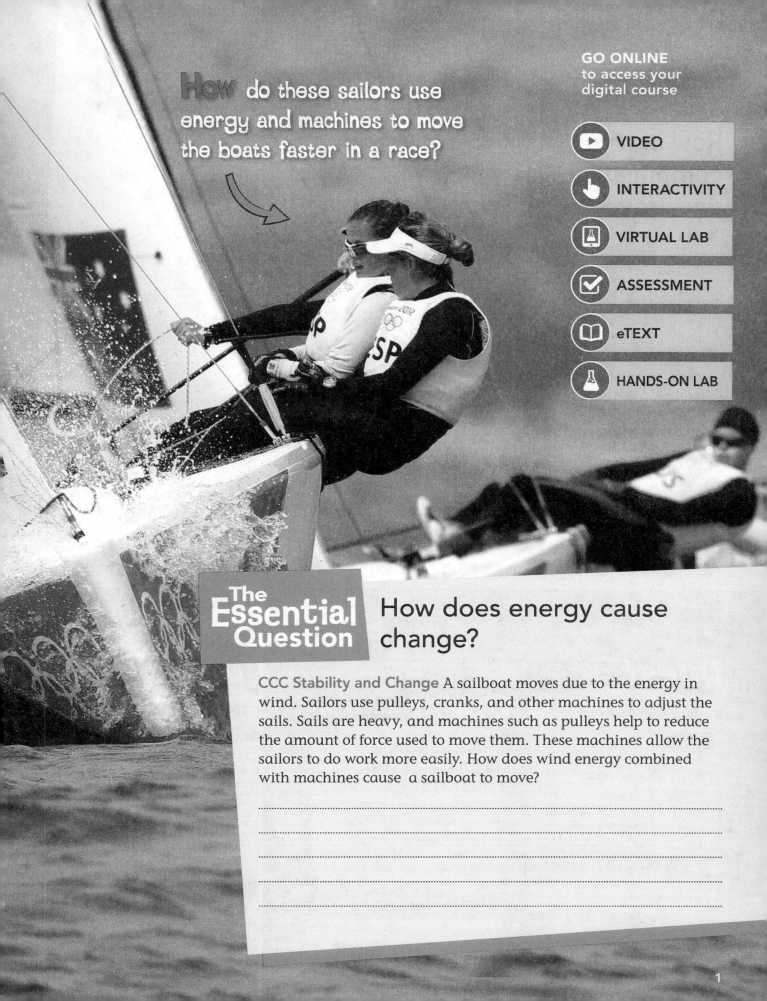

How do these sailors use energy and machines to move the boats faster in a race?

GO ONLINE
to access your
digital course

▶ VIDEO

👆 INTERACTIVITY

🧪 VIRTUAL LAB

☑ ASSESSMENT

📖 eTEXT

⚗ HANDS-ON LAB

The Essential Question

How does energy cause change?

CCC Stability and Change A sailboat moves due to the energy in wind. Sailors use pulleys, cranks, and other machines to adjust the sails. Sails are heavy, and machines such as pulleys help to reduce the amount of force used to move them. These machines allow the sailors to do work more easily. How does wind energy combined with machines cause a sailboat to move?

....

....

....

....

....

Quest KICKOFF

How can you build a complicated machine to do something simple?

NBC LEARN ▶ VIDEO

STEM **Phenomenon** Rube Goldberg™ was a cartoonist and inventor. Goldberg is well-known for his cartoons, which include complex and wacky machines that perform simple tasks. Today, students who study machine design and engineering can participate in contests to build the best Rube Goldberg machine™. Building these machines helps students to understand energy transformations and hone their construction skills. In this Quest, you will design and build a Rube Goldberg machine–an overly complicated machine with a simple end goal. You will use your understanding of energy transformations to construct the chain-reaction machine.

After watching the Quest Kickoff video, answer the following questions.

What simple task might your machine perform?

....
....
....
....

What could be some of the components of the machine?

....
....
....
....

 INTERACTIVITY

Outrageous Energy Contraptions

MS-PS3-2 Develop a model to describe that when the arrangement of objects interacting at a distance changes, different amounts of potential energy are stored in the system.
MS-PS3-5 Construct, use, and present arguments to support the claim that when the kinetic energy of an object changes, energy is transferred to or from the object.

Quest CHECK-IN

IN LESSON 1

STEM How do machines exert force and transfer energy? Develop a design for a chain-reaction machine that can perform a simple task.

 INTERACTIVITY

Applying Energy

Quest CHECK-IN

IN LESSON 2

STEM What are the different types of kinetic energy? Use what you have learned to finalize the design, choose materials, and build your chain-reaction machine.

HANDS-ON LAB

Build a Chain-Reaction Machine

Quest CHECK-IN

IN LESSON 3

STEM What energy transformations take place in a chain-reaction machine? Test your chain-reaction machine prototype and evaluate its performance. Revise and retest it.

HANDS-ON LAB

Test and Evaluate a Chain-Reaction Machine

Many energy transformations occur in this complicated device. In the end, it simply turns on a light bulb!

IN LESSON 4

STEM How can an additional energy transformation improve your design? Modify your chain-reaction machine to include at least one additional energy transformation. Then test, evaluate, and finalize it.

HANDS-ON LAB

Redesign and Retest a Chain-Reaction Machine

Quest FINDINGS

Complete the Quest!

Determine the best way to demonstrate your machine, and show how energy is used in the working of your machine from start to finish.

INTERACTIVITY

Reflect on Your Chain-Reaction Machine

What Would Make a Card Jump?

How can you **use evidence** to make an argument that energy is transformed?

Background

Phenomenon When riding a bike, have you ever thought about what you need to get the bike moving? Or what it takes to stop the bike? Energy is needed to cause an object, such as a bike, to start moving, stop moving, speed up, slow down, or change direction. This energy can be transformed from other kinds of energy. In this activity, you will devise a model to observe energy transformations.

Materials

(per group)
• 3 × 5 index card
• scissors
• rubber band

Safety

Be sure to follow all safety procedures provided by your teacher. The Safety Appendix of your textbook provides more details about the safety icons.

Design a Procedure

1. Using the materials given, you and your partner will devise a model that can demonstrate how energy is transformed. Discuss your ideas with your partner.

2. **SEP Plan a Procedure** Write a procedure that describes how you will use the given materials to construct a model that will allow you to observe energy transformations. Show your procedure to your teacher before you begin.

....
....
....
....
....
....

3. Record your observations.

Observations

HANDS-ON LAB

Connect Go online for a downloadable worksheet of this lab.

Analyze and Conclude

1. **SEP Construct Explanations** Describe what happened to the card in your model.

   ....
   ....
   ....

2. **SEP Engage in Argument** Based on your observations, use evidence to support or refute the argument that energy was transferred from one object to another in your model.

   ....
   ....
   ....
   ....

3. **CCC Energy and Matter** What can you do to increase the potential energy of a rubber band?

   ....
   ....
   ....

1 Energy, Motion, Force, and Work

Guiding Questions

- How is energy related to motion and force?
- What are the relationships among energy, motion, force, and work?

Connections

Literacy Determine Central Ideas

Math Solve Linear Equations

HANDS-ON LAB

ⴈInvestigate Experiment with a soda can to see how an object's energy relates to work.

Vocabulary

energy
motion
force
work
power

Academic Vocabulary

maximum

Connect It !

🖉 **Draw curved arrows on the photograph to represent the motion of the motorcycles.**

SEP Construct Explanations These motorcycles need energy to move. Where does the energy come from?

....

Write Explanatory Texts Describe how the rider exerts a force on the motorcycle.

....

....

SEP Construct Explanations In what way do you think the motorcycles perform work?

....

Energy in Motion and Force

Energy is the ability to do work or cause change. You do work when you pick up your backpack. Motorcycles do work during a race, as in **Figure 1**. The energy to do this work comes from fuel. As the fuel burns, it changes into other substances and releases energy.

Energy comes in many forms. Light, sound, and electricity are all forms of energy. Energy can also be transferred from place to place. For example, chemical energy is transferred from the food you eat to your body. Energy from the sun is transferred to Earth in the form of electromagnetic radiation. Energy is not something you can see directly. You can, however, observe its effects. When you touch something hot, you don't see the energy, but you feel the heat. You can hear the sound of a bass drum, but you can't see the sound energy itself.

Energy and Motion It takes energy for motion to occur. An object is in **motion** if its position changes relative to another object. A pitched ball would not speed toward home plate without energy supplied by the pitcher. Energy supplied by food enables a racehorse to run around a track. Energy stored in gasoline allows the motorcycles in **Figure 1** to move at high speeds. In each of these examples, the more energy that is used, the faster the object can move.

VIDEO

Watch this video to better understand energy.

Reflect Think about the different methods you used to travel from one place to another today. In your science notebook, describe two of these ways. For each, identify the energy source that caused the movement.

Racing Around the Track
Figure 1 Energy, motion, force, and work are all involved in a motorcycle race.

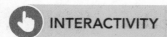
Energy and Force The relationship between energy and motion also involves forces. A **force** is a push or pull. You can see many examples of this relationship on a construction site. Look at **Figure 2** and study the examples of how energy is used to apply a force that causes motion.

✓ READING CHECK **Explain** How would you describe a force?

....

....

Force

Figure 2 When energy is used to apply force, objects can move.

CCC Energy and Matter ✏ Draw an arrow on each numbered picture to show the direction of the force being applied. Then label each arrow with "push" or "pull" to identify the type of force being applied.

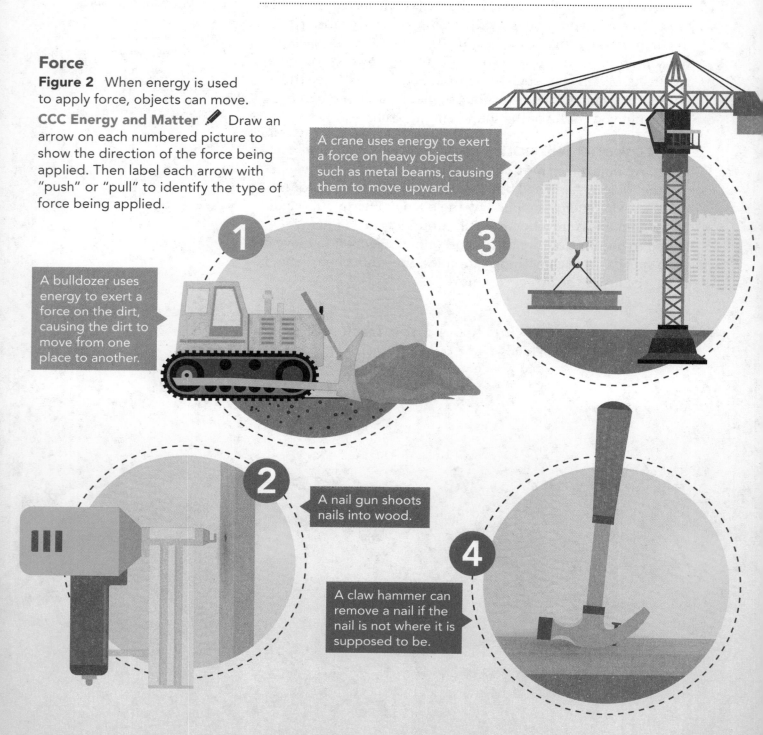

A bulldozer uses energy to exert a force on the dirt, causing the dirt to move from one place to another.

A crane uses energy to exert a force on heavy objects such as metal beams, causing them to move upward.

A nail gun shoots nails into wood.

A claw hammer can remove a nail if the nail is not where it is supposed to be.

Force and Work

You might think of "work" as a job, such as teaching, being a doctor, or bagging groceries at the local supermarket. But the scientific meaning of work is much broader than that. In scientific terms, you do **work** any time you exert a force on an object that causes the object to change its motion in the same direction in which you exert the force. All of the machines on the previous page show work being done because the forces are being applied in the same direction as the motion shown.

You probably carry your books from one class to another every school day. You know that you exert a force on the books as you carry them. However, you do very little work on them because of the direction of the force exerted. When you carry an object while walking at constant speed in a straight line, you exert an upward force on the object. Because the force is vertical and the motion is horizontal, you don't do any work on the object itself.

Figure 3 shows three different ways to move a tool bin. The weight of the bin is the same in each situation, but the amount of work varies. For a given force, the **maximum** amount of work is done when both the movement and the force are in the same direction.

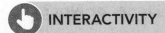
INTERACTIVITY

Explore how levers work in this virtual activity.

Academic Vocabulary

Write a synonym for maximum.

....

Force, Motion, and Work

Figure 3 ✏ The amount of work that you do on something depends on the direction of the applied force and the object's motion. In the second and third pictures, label each arrow with "motion" or "force."

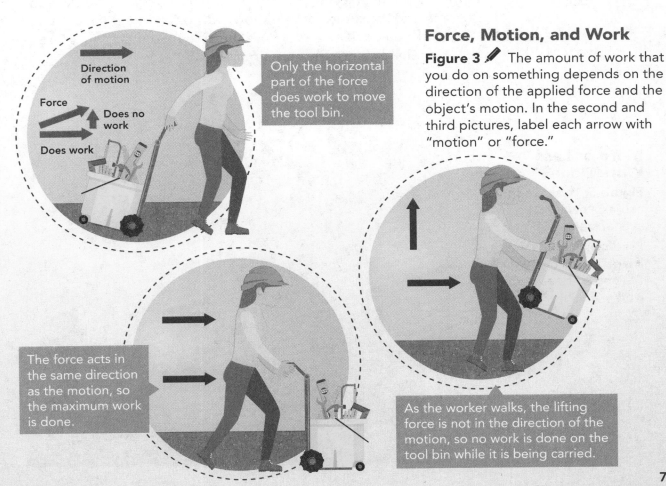

Direction of motion

Force

Does no work

Does work

Only the horizontal part of the force does work to move the tool bin.

The force acts in the same direction as the motion, so the maximum work is done.

As the worker walks, the lifting force is not in the direction of the motion, so no work is done on the tool bin while it is being carried.

Work Done, or Not?

Figure 4 This girl struggles to open a jar, but the lid does not budge.

SEP Construct Explanations Is the girl doing work? Explain your reasoning.

....

....

....

....

....

👆 INTERACTIVITY

Explore how energy is needed to get an object to move, and discover how work on an object affects its motion.

Work Requires Motion

Imagine that you are trying to open a jar, and the lid is stuck. You exert a lot of force on the lid, but it doesn't move. Are you doing work? No. No matter how much force you exert, you don't do any work if the lid does not move.

Calculating Work

Suppose you bought a new painting for your room. You have to carry the painting up three porch steps to the first floor and then up another flight of 12 steps to the second floor. (See **Figure 5**.) Is it more work to lift the painting up 12 steps than three steps? As you might guess, moving an object a greater distance requires more work than moving the same object a shorter distance. The amount of work you do depends on both the amount of force you exert and the distance the object moves.

More or Less Work Done?

Figure 5 This person carries a painting up two sets of steps.

Predict 🖊 Circle the image in which you think the person does more work.

The amount of work done on an object is calculated by multiplying force times distance. When force is measured in newtons and distance in meters, the SI unit of work is the newton-meter (N-m). This unit is also called a joule (J). One joule is the amount of work you do when you exert a force of 1 newton to move an object a distance of 1 meter.

✓ READING CHECK **Determine Central Ideas** What two factors affect how much work is done in any given action?

....

Math Toolbox

Calculating Work

A grandfather lifts a baby 1.5 m with an upward force of 80 N, as shown in the third photograph below. You can use the relationship among work, force, and distance to find out how much work is done:

Work = Force × Distance
Work = 80 N × 1.5 m
Work = 120 N-m

The amount of work done is 120 N-m, or 120 J.

Use the formula for finding work to answer questions 1–2. Show your calculations. Use joules as the unit for work.

1. Solve Linear Equations This woman lifts a plant 2 m with a force of 65 N. How much work does she do?

....

2. Calculate How much work is done when 300 N of force is used to lift the dog 1.5 m?

....

3. Classify Label the photos below with the words *least, medium,* and *most* to rank them from least work done to most work done.

9

☑Investigate Experiment with a soda can to see how an object's energy relates to work.

Work Related to Energy and Power

Did you pull your shoes from the closet this morning? If so, then you did work on the shoes. As you have read, work is done when a force moves an object in the direction of the force. When an object moves, its position changes. What causes change? Recall that the ability to do work or cause change is called energy. Energy is measured in joules—the same units as work.

When you do work on an object, some of your energy is transferred to that object. Think about the plant shown in the Math Toolbox. When the gardener lifted the plant to the high shelf, she transferred energy to the plant.

If you carry a bag of groceries up a flight of stairs, the work you do is the same whether you walk or run. The time it takes to do the work does not affect the amount of work you do on an object. But something else—power—is affected. **Power** is the rate at which work is done, and it equals the amount of work done on an object in a unit of time. You can think of power in two main ways. An object that has more power than another object does more work in the same amount of time. It can also mean doing the same amount of work in less time. Look at **Figure 6** for other examples that compare power.

Work and Power
Figure 6 In each of these images, work is being done. For each image, give two examples of ways the people shown can increase the power being used.

These people load 10 items on the truck in 10 minutes. Ways power can be increased:

....

This person mows half of her backyard in one hour. Ways power can be increased:

....

Calculating Power

All you need to know to calculate power is how much and how quickly work is being done. Power is calculated by dividing the amount of work done by the amount of time it takes to do the work. This can be written as the following formula:

$$\text{Power} = \frac{\text{Work}}{\text{Time}}$$

Because work is equal to force times distance, you can rewrite the equation for power as follows:

$$\text{Power} = \frac{\text{Force} \times \text{Distance}}{\text{Time}}$$

When work is measured in joules and time in seconds, the SI unit of power is the watt (W). One watt equals one joule per second (1 W = 1 J/s). Examine **Figure 7** to learn more about calculating power.

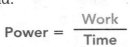

INTERACTIVITY

Examine real-world examples of energy transformations and forces.

Power

Figure 7 Most climbers of the Himalayan Mountains would not make it to the peaks without the help of Sherpas.

SEP Use Mathematics Sherpas are natives of Nepal, and they carry heavy loads of equipment up the mountains for the climbers. Suppose one Sherpa uses a force of 980 N to move a load of equipment to a height of 20 meters in 25 seconds. How much power is used?

Different Types of Power

Figure 8 Leaf blowers require gasoline for power, while rakes require power from your body.

Power and Energy

Recall that power is the rate at which work is done. Power is also the rate at which energy is transferred, or the amount of energy transferred in a unit of time.

$$Power = \frac{Energy\ transferred}{Time}$$

For example, a 60-watt lightbulb transfers 60 joules of energy per second. Different machines have different amounts of power. For instance, you can use either a rake or a leaf blower to remove leaves from your lawn (see **Figure 8**). Each tool transfers the same amount of energy to the leaves when it moves leaves the same distance. However, the leaf blower moves leaves faster than the rake. The leaf blower has more power because it transfers the same amount of energy to the leaves in less time.

✓ READING CHECK Apply Concepts What is the difference in power between a 60-watt lightbulb and a 100-watt lightbulb?

....

Model It

SEP Develop Models ✏ In the concept map below, label each line to show how energy, motion, force, work, and power relate to each other. One line is labeled for you as an example.

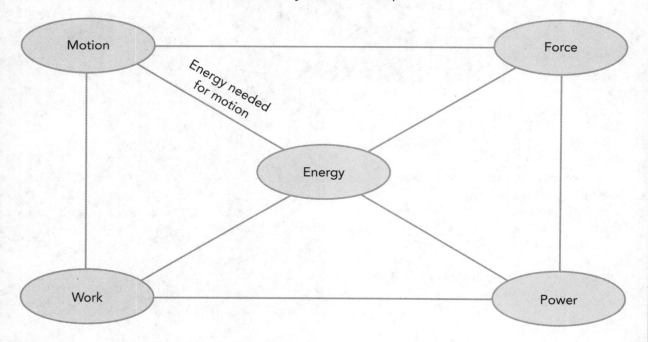

☑ LESSON 1 Check

1. **Explain** How are energy and motion related?

....

....

....

2. **Apply Concepts** Give an example in which energy produces a force that causes motion.

....

....

....

....

3. **SEP Engage in Argument** Is work done when you hold a heavy object for a long time? Why or why not?

....

....

....

....

4. **SEP Use Mathematics** What force was applied to an object if 35 J of work was done and the object moved 7 m? Show your work.

....

....

....

....

5. **SEP Ask Questions** A student did 24 J of work on a chair. She applied a force of 12 N and moved the chair 2 m. What question do you need to ask to determine the amount of power used?

....

....

6. **CCC Cause and Effect** 🖊 Use the terms *motion*, *power*, and *work* to complete the table.

Cause	Effect
Energy transferred over time	
Force applied to an object to change its position	
Force moving an object over a distance	

Quest CHECK-IN

In this lesson, you learned about the basics of energy and how force and motion relate to it. You also learned about how these concepts relate to how work is done.

SEP Define Problems How do the concepts of energy, force, and motion relate to the machine you will be designing? What factors will you need to consider in your design?

....

....

....

....

....

👆 **INTERACTIVITY**

Applying Energy

Go online to learn about how energy, force, and motion relate to machines. Then, develop the design for your machine.

Kinetic Energy and Potential Energy

Guiding Questions

- What determines an object's kinetic energy?
- What factors affect potential energy?
- What is the relationship between potential and kinetic energy?

Connections

Literacy Integrate With Visuals

Math Evaluate Expressions

MS-PS3-1, MS-PS3-2

HANDS-ON LAB

иInvestigate Use a skateboard to model changes in kinetic energy.

Vocabulary

kinetic energy
potential energy
gravitational
    potential
    energy
elastic potential
    energy

Academic Vocabulary

virtue

Connect It !

✎ **Draw an arrow on the image to show the direction that you think the rocks and dirt are moving.**

SEP Construct Explanations It takes a lot of energy to move this amount of dirt and rocks. What do you think is the source of this energy?

....

....

Apply Scientific Reasoning What is another example of something that starts moving suddenly?

....

....

Kinetic Energy

Study the landslide shown in **Figure 1**. In this image, dirt and rocks are moving rapidly down the side of the hill. As you read in Lesson 1, it takes energy to cause the motion you see in this photo. When objects are in motion, they are demonstrating a certain kind of energy—kinetic energy. **Kinetic energy** is the energy that an object possesses by **virtue** of being in motion.

Examples of kinetic energy are all around us. A car moving down a road exhibits kinetic energy. So does a runner participating in a race. As you sit at your desk in school, you exhibit kinetic energy every time you turn a page in a book or type on a keyboard.

Factors Affecting Kinetic Energy The kinetic energy of an object depends on both its speed and its mass. The faster an object moves, the more kinetic energy it has. For example, if a tennis ball moves at great speed, it has more kinetic energy than if the ball had been softly lobbed over the net. Kinetic energy also increases as mass increases. A wheelbarrow full of dirt has more kinetic energy than an empty wheelbarrow has, due to its greater mass.

INTERACTIVITY

Interpret graphs to understand the relationships among a snowboarder's kinetic energy, mass, and speed.

Academic Vocabulary

The phrase *by virtue of* means "because of." In what other way have you heard the term virtue used?

....

....

....

Landslide!
Figure 1 A landslide is a sudden movement of rock and soil. Before the landslide, all the rocks and soil were in place and not moving.

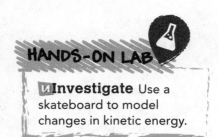

HANDS-ON LAB

Investigate Use a skateboard to model changes in kinetic energy.

READING CHECK

Apply Concepts
Underline the unit of energy you get when you calculate kinetic energy.

Calculating Kinetic Energy

Keeping in mind that the kinetic energy of an object depends on its mass and its speed, you can use the following equation to solve for the kinetic energy of an object:

$$\text{Kinetic energy} = \frac{1}{2} \times \text{Mass} \times \text{Speed}^2$$

The exponent "2" that follows "Speed" tells you that the speed is multiplied by itself first.

For example, suppose a girl with a mass of 50 kg is jogging at a speed of 2 meters per second (m/s). Note that $1 \text{kg} \cdot \text{m}^2/\text{s}^2 = 1$ joule (J).

$$
\begin{aligned}
\text{Kinetic energy of girl} &= \frac{1}{2} \times 50 \text{ kg} \times (2 \text{ m/s})^2 \\
&= \frac{1}{2} \times 50 \text{ kg} \times (2 \text{ m/s} \times 2 \text{ m/s}) \\
&= \frac{1}{2} \times 50 \text{ kg} \times 4 \text{ m}^2/\text{s}^2 \\
&= 100 \text{ kg} \cdot \text{m}^2/\text{s}^2 = 100 \text{ J}
\end{aligned}
$$

Do changes in speed and mass both have the same effect on kinetic energy? Use the Math Toolbox to answer this question.

Math Toolbox

Mass, Speed, and Kinetic Energy

A boy and his dogs are running.
The white dog has a mass of 10 kg.
The black dog has a mass of 20 kg.
The boy has a mass of 40 kg.
They are all running at 3 m/s.

1. **Evaluate Expressions** Determine the kinetic energy of the dogs and the boy. Record the kinetic energy for each.

....

....

2. **Construct Graphs** 🖊 Graph the data to show how mass and kinetic energy are related.

3. **SEP Use Mathematics** Suppose the smaller dog speeds up to 6 m/s. What is the kinetic energy of the dog now? How is kinetic energy related to speed?

....

....

Kinetic Energy Versus Mass

(graph: y-axis "Kinetic energy (J)" from 0 to 250 in increments of 50; x-axis "Mass (kg)" from 0 to 50 in increments of 10)

Potential Energy

Kinetic energy is easy to observe because there is motion involved. But an object that is not moving may still have energy. Some objects have energy simply as a result of their shapes or positions. Energy that results from the position or shape of an object is called **potential energy**. This type of energy has the potential to transform into kinetic energy, or, in other words, to do work. Recall that work involves using force to move an object over a distance.

When you raise a bottle up to your mouth to take a drink of water, or when you stretch out a rubber band, you transfer energy to the object. The energy you transfer is stored, or held in readiness by the object. It may be used later if the bottle is dropped or the rubber band is released (see **Figure 2**).

Look back again at the photo of the landslide at the beginning of the lesson. You see the dirt and rocks moving, showing kinetic energy. At some point before the photo was taken, however, the dirt and rocks were not yet moving. At that stage, they held potential energy.

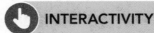

INTERACTIVITY

Investigate model racecars to see how mass affects kinetic energy.

Literacy Connection

Integrate With Visuals
In your notebook, draw an object with elastic potential energy.

Stored-Up Energy

Figure 2 This stretched rubber band is not moving, but it still contains energy—potential energy. Once the fingers that are stretching the rubber band release the band, what kind of energy will the rubber band have?

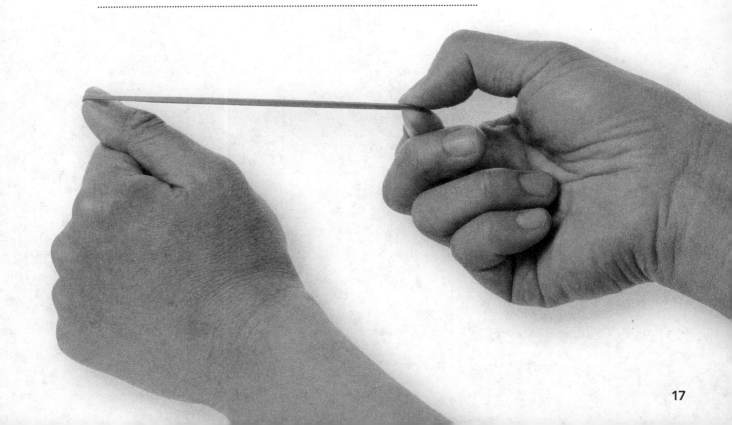

▶ VIDEO

Explore gravitational potential energy on Earth and on the moon.

HANDS-ON LAB

☑**Investigate** Develop a model with magnets to show how the arrangement of objects affects potential energy.

Gravitational Potential Energy

Figure 3 A cyclist sitting still at the top of a hill displays gravitational potential energy. What makes it possible for the cyclist to have this type of energy?

....
....
....
....

Gravitational Potential Energy
There are two types of potential energy directly related to kinetic energy. One of these types is **gravitational potential energy**. This type of potential energy is related to an object's vertical position—how high it is above the ground. The potential energy is stored as a result of the gravitational pull of Earth on the object.

Gravitational potential energy can be measured by the amount of work needed to lift an object to a certain height. Remember that work is equal to force multiplied by distance. The force you use to lift the object is equal to its weight. Weight is the force that gravity exerts on an object. The distance you move the object is its height above ground level. You can calculate an object's gravitational potential energy using this equation:

**Gravitational potential energy =
Weight × Height above ground**

For example, suppose a cat has a weight of 40 newtons, which is about 9 pounds. The cat is lifted 2 meters off the ground. You can calculate its potential energy:

Gravitational potential energy = 40 N × 2 m

= 80 N-m, or 80 J

The energy of the cyclist at the top of hill shown in **Figure 3** is another example of gravitational potential energy.

Elastic Potential Energy

Sometimes, an object has a different type of potential energy due to its shape. **Elastic potential energy** is the energy associated with objects that can be compressed or stretched. This type of potential energy can be stored in such items as rubber bands, bungee cords, springs, and an arrow drawn into a bow.

Trampolines also store elastic potential energy. Take a look at **Figure 4**. When the girl presses down on the trampoline, the trampoline changes shape. The trampoline now has elastic potential energy. When the girl jumps up off the trampoline, this stored energy is transferred from the trampoline to the girl, sending the girl upward. During this energy transfer, the elastic potential energy of the trampoline is transformed into different types of energy.

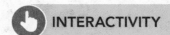

INTERACTIVITY

Explore the potential energy of roller coasters.

✓ READING CHECK **Integrate With Visuals** Explain your rankings of the trampoline's potential energy.

....

....

....

Elastic Potential Energy

Figure 4 The energy stored in a stretched object, such as a trampoline, is elastic potential energy. Rank the amount of elastic potential energy of the trampoline from greatest to least using the words *most*, *medium* and *least*. Write your answers in the boxes next to the images.

MS-PS3-1, MS-PS3-2

1. **Explain Phenomena** Explain why a running deer has kinetic energy.

....

....

....

2. **SEP Use Mathematics** Imagine the running deer has a mass of 100 kg and is running at a speed of 8 m/s. What is the deer's kinetic energy, in joules?

....

....

3. **SEP Construct Explanations** Several people are using bows to shoot arrows at targets. At what point do the bows have elastic potential energy? At what point do the arrows have kinetic energy?

....

....

....

....

....

....

....

4. **SEP Use Mathematics** Imagine that a bowling ball needs to be lifted 1.5 meters, and its gravitational potential energy is 90 joules. How much does the bowling ball weigh?

....

....

....

5. **Determine Differences** What is the main difference between gravitational potential energy and elastic potential energy?

....

....

....

....

....

....

....

....

....

....

....

Quest CHECK-IN

In this lesson, you learned about potential and kinetic energy and the different roles they play with regard to forces and motion in everyday life.

SEP Define Problems How might the concepts of potential and kinetic energy impact the design of your machine? What factors do you need to consider?

....

....

....

....

HANDS-ON LAB

Build a Chain-Reaction Machine

Go online to download the lab worksheet. Finalize the design for your machine, choose construction materials, and build it! Then, analyze the moving parts of your machine and identify the different types of energy that come into play.

Prosthetics on the Move

INTERACTIVITY

Discover the properties of materials and changes in energy to guide your construction of a prosthetic limb.

How might you design a prosthetic arm that meets the needs of a modern, on-the-go person? You engineer it!

The Challenge: To design a prosthetic arm based on research into current prosthetic technology.

Phenomenon Until very recently, prosthetics, or artificial limbs, were made of wood, rubber, or plastic. These older prosthetics were solid and heavy, and they often made movement difficult.

When you walk, your foot muscles and leg muscles provide the force to push off the ground. The potential energy stored in your body becomes the kinetic energy of motion. Using an artificial leg, however, takes practice and can be uncomfortable because other muscles strain to carry the artificial limb.

Prosthetic design has advanced thanks to new technologies. In the early 2000s, engineers developed a carbon prosthetic for track athletes. This flexible leg bends and provides elastic potential energy to help the athlete run. The lighter weight of the materials allows the runner to move more efficiently with less muscle strain. Today, advanced engineers are working on limbs that are controlled by the electrical impulses in the human brain, mimicking the way our brains signal our muscles to move!

This prosthetic leg has the shape, weight, and flexibility to allow this runner to sprint again!

DESIGN CHALLENGE How can you design and build a new kind of prosthetic limb? Go to the Engineering Design Notebook to find out!

21

Other Forms of Energy

Guiding Questions

- How can different forms of energy be classified, quantified, and measured?
- How are different forms of energy related to each other?

Connection

Literacy Cite Textual Evidence

MS-PS3-5

HANDS-ON LAB

u**Investigate** Observe the different types of energy at play when you use a flashlight.

Vocabulary

mechanical energy
nuclear energy
thermal energy
chemical energy
electrical energy
electromagnetic radiation

Academic Vocabulary

medium

Connect It !

✎ Circle and label the parts of the drone that are similar to the parts of the hummingbird.

Infer   What kinds of energy provide power to the drone and to the hummingbird?

....

....

....

Determining Mechanical Energy

The term *mechanical* may make you think of images of metal machines or a mechanic tinkering under the hood of a car. In science, *mechanical* is an adjective that refers to things that are or can be in motion, which covers just about any object we can think of, from particles all the way up to Earth itself. **Mechanical energy** is the energy an object has due to its motion, shape, position, or a combination of these factors.

An object's mechanical energy equals the total of its kinetic and potential energy. For example, a train chugging uphill has energy, and much of that energy is energy of motion—kinetic energy. But a train that is sitting idle at the top of a hill also has energy—potential energy. By adding these two energy forms together, you can determine the train's mechanical energy:

Mechanical Energy = Potential Energy + **Kinetic Energy**

☑ READING CHECK **Cite Textual Evidence** What are the three factors that determine an object's mechanical energy?

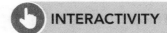

INTERACTIVITY

Discover several different types of energy.

Inspired by Nature

Figure 1 Engineers often look to nature for inspiration for their machines. This drone has features similar to those of the hummingbird, and they both need energy to function.

INTERACTIVITY

Investigate forms of energy involved with roller coasters and high divers.

▶ VIDEO

Learn more about nuclear energy.

Literacy Connection

Cite Textual Evidence
As you read about different forms of energy, underline the types of evidence that can help you identify those different forms.

More Forms of Energy

Much of the energy that you observe is mechanical energy, but energy can take many other forms as well. Some other forms of energy are associated with tiny particles, such as atoms and molecules, that make up objects. These forms include nuclear energy, thermal energy, chemical energy, electric energy, and electromagnetic energy.

Nuclear Energy All matter is made of particles called atoms. The center of the atom is called the nucleus (plural: nuclei). **Nuclear energy** is a type of potential energy stored in the nucleus. It can be released through a nuclear reaction. In one type of nuclear reaction, called fission, a nucleus splits into smaller fragments. When it breaks apart, it releases energy (**Figure 2**). If fission reactions are controlled, the release of energy can be used to generate electricity. Nuclear power plants harness nuclear energy for this purpose.

Fusion is another type of nuclear reaction. In fusion, small nuclei combine to form larger nuclei. One place that fusion happens is inside the sun. Some of the energy released by this reaction makes its way to Earth as light. Fusion releases more energy than fission, but the extremely high temperatures that are required to start a fusion reaction make it more difficult to use and control.

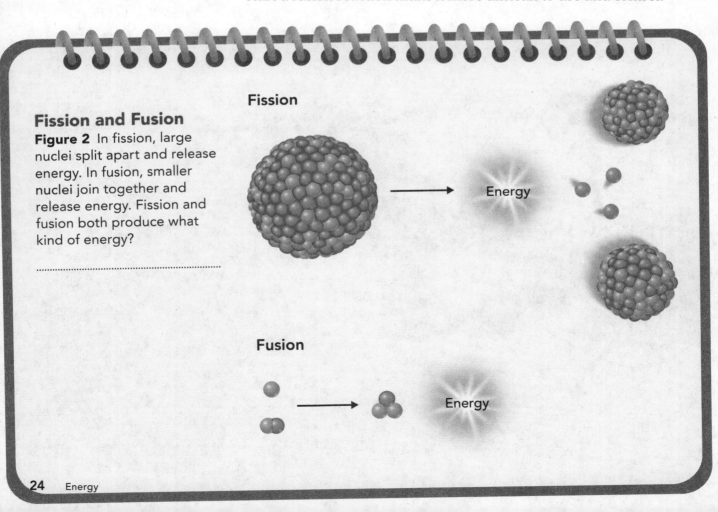

Fission and Fusion
Figure 2 In fission, large nuclei split apart and release energy. In fusion, smaller nuclei join together and release energy. Fission and fusion both produce what kind of energy?

....

Hot-Air Balloon
Figure 3 The left circle shows how densely packed the air particles are in the air outside the balloon.

SEP Use Models
Read about thermal energy below. Then, in the empty circle, draw an illustration representing the particles of the warmer air inside the balloon.

Thermal Energy

The total potential and kinetic energy of particles in an object is called **thermal energy**. Lots of particle movement means lots of kinetic energy, and that means a high temperature. Think of a pot of boiling water. The particles are moving very quickly, which results in a high temperature. This means the water has a lot of thermal energy. If the water is then put in the freezer, its kinetic energy will decrease. When its kinetic energy decreases, its thermal energy and temperature also decrease.

The transfer of energy into the thermal energy of an object is called heat. Heat flows from a hotter object to a cooler one through a combination of processes. These processes are called conduction, convection, and radiation. Most substances expand, or take up more space, when heated. When they lose heat, they contract and take up less space. The effect of heat allows a hot air balloon to rise. A flame heats the air inside the hot-air balloon, giving the particles more thermal energy (**Figure 3**). Since they have more thermal energy, they move faster and spread apart. The air in the balloon is then less dense than the air outside the balloon, so the balloon rises.

HANDS-ON LAB

Investigate Observe the different types of energy at play when you use a flashlight.

Chemical Energy What type of energy is in the food you eat, in the cells of your body, and in the substances that make a lightstick glow? It is called **chemical energy**. Chemical energy is a form of potential energy because it results from the relative positions of the particles within a material. The particles are held in those positions by chemical bonds. When these bonds are broken, energy is released.

Plants produce a form of stored chemical energy when they perform photosynthesis. In this process, plants take in energy from sunlight. They also take in water and carbon dioxide. Plant cells break the bonds of water and carbon dioxide to produce sugars. Those sugars store chemical energy. The plant later breaks the bonds of the sugar to release the chemical energy on which it lives. Similarly, your body breaks bonds of sugar from your food. Energy is released when your body breaks bonds that hold the sugar molecules together. Your body uses that energy to power your cells.

Petroleum, or oil, is another source of chemical energy. Oil is converted into gasoline and diesel fuel, which contain potential energy in the form of chemical bonds. When fuel is burned in engines, the energy in these fuels can be used to makes cars run.

Reflect What have you heard about the pros and cons of using oil for energy? In your science notebook, describe what you have heard, and write down your own conclusions about the burning of oil.

Question It !

1. **Draw Conclusions** Batteries allow us to store energy for when it's needed, such as starting a car engine or jump-starting another car whose battery has lost its charge. But batteries cannot operate without chemical reactions. What kind of energy do you think is stored in the substances within the battery?

....

2. **Reason Abstractly** When someone jump-starts a car, what do you think happens to the stored energy in the working battery?

....
....
....
....

Electrical Energy

Electrical energy is the form of energy most of us use to power devices such as lights, computers, and audio systems. **Electrical energy** is the energy of electric charges. Different materials, and even particles, can have different charges. These differences in charge can result in the movement of electrical charge—a type of kinetic energy called electricity. When charges are not moving but are near one another, they have electric potential energy. This energy can be converted to electricity.

Electromagnetic Radiation

Visible light is one type of electromagnetic radiation. **Electromagnetic radiation** is a form of kinetic energy that travels through space in waves. It does not need a **medium**, such as air or water, to travel through. This is why you can see the stars even though outer space does not contain a medium. Our world has a wide variety of electromagnetic energy, from X-rays that produce images of bones to microwaves that heat leftover food or transmit signals between mobile phones and towers. Other types of electromagnetic radiation include ultraviolet (UV) waves, infrared (or heat) waves, and radio waves. Like other forms of kinetic energy, all types of electromagnetic radiation can transform into thermal energy when heating something.

Academic Vocabulary

In your reading here, the word medium is used to indicate a substance through which a force acts. What are some other meanings of medium that you use or hear in everyday life?

....

....

....

....

....

☑ READING CHECK **Classifying Forms of Energy** 🖍

Sort electromagnetic radiation, mechanical energy, electrical energy, thermal energy, chemical energy, and nuclear energy into one of the three categories in the diagram.

Potential Energy   **Both**   **Kinetic Energy**

Energy at the Cookout

Figure 4 Many objects in this scene contain more than one form of energy.

1. **Claim** 🖊 Label this scene with as many forms of energy as you can find.

2. **Evidence** 🖊 Draw a star next to an object that contains more than one form of energy and explain your reasoning below.

....

....

3. Reasoning The grill converts chemical energy from propane into thermal energy that heats food. What is another example of an energy change in this image?

....

....

....

....

....

MS-PS3-5

1. **SEP Use Mathematics** At a certain point, the kinetic energy of a falling basketball is 30.8 J and its potential energy is 16.0 J. What is its mechanical energy?

....

2. **Identify** Which type of nuclear energy involves splitting atoms?

....

3. **Represent Relationships** What are some of the relationships among thermal energy, kinetic energy, particle movement, and temperature?

....

....

....

....

....

4. **SEP Construct Explanations** What type(s) of energy do you acquire when you eat a bowl of hot vegetable soup? Explain.

....

....

....

5. **SEP Engage in Argument** Why do we say the particles in a rock lying on the ground have kinetic energy and potential energy?

....

....

....

....

....

....

Quest CHECK-IN

In this lesson, you learned about other forms of energy, such as nuclear energy and electromagnetic radiation. You also started to think about how these forms of energy can change into other forms, and how to tell when such a change has occurred.

Evaluate Why do engineers need to keep track of potential and kinetic energy and energy transformations in prototypes of machines?

....

....

....

....

HANDS-ON LAB

Test and Evaluate a Chain-Reaction Machine

Go online to download the lab worksheet. Test your chain-reaction machine prototype and evaluate its performance. Then revise your machine's design and retest as needed. Think about energy transformations that are taking place and the roles of potential and kinetic energy.

Energy Engineer

Reinventing
ENERGY SYSTEMS

We all use energy every moment of our lives. It lights our classrooms, runs our computers, and powers our industries. For much of the twentieth century, the United States depended largely on fossil fuels for energy. This has been changing in recent decades because the supply of fossil fuels is limited, and excessive use of these fuels has caused environmental damage on a vast scale. Today, people are turning more and more to renewable sources of fuel, such as solar and wind power. This is where the energy engineers play a role.

The purpose of an energy engineer's job is simple: to make the world more energy-efficient. Energy engineers carry out a wide range of work that involves research, design, and construction.

Some energy engineers explore new methods of obtaining energy, while others develop ways to integrate renewable energy sources into the existing power grid. Energy engineers also work with architects to incorporate clean energy sources in new construction. Additionally, some of these engineers help to develop more efficient machinery, such as cars that run on alternative fuels.

This type of work involves mathematics, physics, and chemistry. It offers creative challenges and a wide variety of tasks. If you enjoy these subjects and challenges, this career might be right for you!

▶ **VIDEO**

Learn about the work an energy engineer does.

MY CAREER

Speak with an energy engineer at a local laboratory or office to learn more about this career.

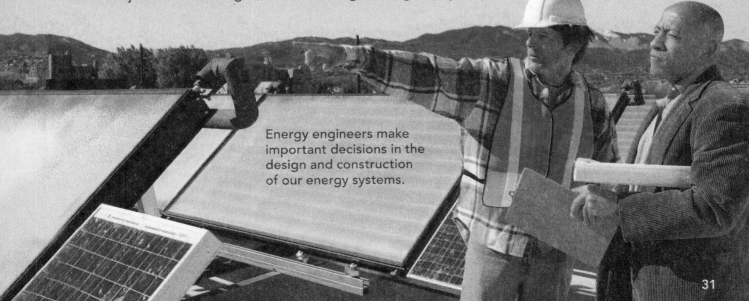

Energy engineers make important decisions in the design and construction of our energy systems.

Energy Change and Conservation

Guiding Questions

- In what ways can energy change from one form to another?
- How is energy transferred?
- How does the law of conservation of energy apply to transformations and transfers?

Connections

Literacy Cite Textual Evidence

Math Use Ratio Relationships

MS-PS3-5

HANDS-ON LAB

uInvestigate Explore how the changing kinetic energy of a bouncing ball is related to conservation of energy.

Vocabulary

law of conservation of energy

Academic Vocabulary

pivot

Connect It !

✏ **Trace the movement of the snowboarder.**

Infer How is the snowboarder able to soar through the air?

....

....

....

Energy Changes Form

All forms of energy can be transformed into other forms of energy. Energy can transform once (which we call a single transformation) or multiple times. A toaster provides a good example of a single transformation. Electrical energy passes through metal wires and is transformed into thermal energy.

If you eat toast, the resulting process is an example of multiple transformations. Your body transforms chemical energy stored in cells into the kinetic energy that moves your mouth. Your digestive system uses mechanical and chemical energy to digest the bread. Some of the chemical energy in the bread is released as thermal energy that helps your body maintain its temperature. Some of the remaining chemical energy is delivered back to your body's cells. The cells then transform that chemical energy into mechanical energy that allows your body to function.

Multiple transformations also go into the making of the bread. Sunlight, which is a form of electromagnetic radiation, is harnessed by wheat plants to create chemical energy. Mechanical energy is used to grind the wheat into flour. The flour is combined with water and yeast to make dough—more chemical energy. As the dough is baked in the oven, electrical energy is used to increase the thermal energy of the oven. Heat is transferred from the oven to the dough, and the thermal energy of the dough increases as it bakes into bread. Many of the processes that we rely on daily involve multiple transformations.

Literacy Connection

Cite Textual Evidence
What evidence in the text supports the claim that energy changes form? List two examples.

....

....

....

....

....

....

Snowboard Jumping
Figure 1 The snowboarder thrusts up and forward by using her legs. But most of the energy that allows her to travel a great distance through the air is supplied by something else.

Kinetic and Potential Energy

One common energy transformation involves potential energy changing to kinetic energy. The snowboarder on the previous page had potential energy when she stood at the top of the hill. As she pushed herself off the top, gravity transformed the potential energy into kinetic energy. As she accelerated down the hill, the potential energy declined while the kinetic energy increased This is true of any falling object, such as the ball in **Figure 2**. Recall that the weight of an object and its height above the ground are proportionally related to its gravitational potential energy. And so, as the height of the ball decreases, it loses potential energy while gaining kinetic energy. The ball's kinetic energy is greatest right before it hits the ground.

A pendulum also demonstrates the relationship between kinetic and potential energy. A pendulum consists of something with mass suspended on an arm or pole that swings back and forth from a **pivot** point. A swinging boat ride at an amusement park is a kind of pendulum (**Figure 3**). At its highest point, the pendulum has no movement and therefore no kinetic energy. When it begins to swing down, potential energy declines as the kinetic energy increases. The kinetic energy and the speed of the pendulum are greatest at the bottom, or midpoint, of the swing. As the pendulum swings upward, it loses kinetic energy and gains potential energy until it is motionless again and ready to swing back to the other side.

Academic Vocabulary

The term pivot is often used in describing the action of basketball players when they keep one foot firmly in place while moving their other foot. What other things in everyday life might pivot?

....

....

....

Falling Objects

Figure 2 ✏ As an object falls, its potential energy decreases while its kinetic energy increases. Circle the location where the ball has the most kinetic energy.

Pendulum Physics

Figure 3 This amusement park ride is basically a pendulum.

Use Models ✏ Use the abbreviation *PE* for potential energy and *KE* for kinetic energy to label the positions where the boat has maximum PE, minimum PE, maximum KE, and minimum KE.

Energy Transformation and Transfer

Energy transformation and energy transfer sometimes occur in the same process at the same time, but they are not the same thing. Energy transformation occurs when one form of energy changes into another. The potential energy of a pendulum, such as the wrecking ball in **Figure 4**, transforms into kinetic energy as it falls due to the force of gravity. Energy transfer takes place when energy moves from one object to another. When the wrecking ball hits the wall, some of the kinetic energy of the ball transfers to the wall, causing the wall to fall over. As the wrecking ball swings, energy is also transferred from the ball to the air, due to the force of friction. In this case, energy transfers, but it is also transformed. Some of the mechanical energy of the moving wrecking ball is transferred and transformed into thermal energy of the surrounding air. Whenever a moving object experiences friction, some of its mechanical energy is transformed into thermal energy.

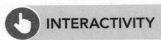

INTERACTIVITY

Explore different examples of energy transformations.

✓ **READING CHECK** **Cite Textual Evidence** Underline the sentences that explain the difference between energy transformation and energy transfer.

Model It!

Transformation and Transfer in Demolition

Figure 4 🖉 Draw pictures in the empty boxes to show what happens as the wrecking ball swings. Describe the energy transformations and transfers that are occurring.

Ball at top of swing	Ball at bottom of swing	Ball hitting the wall

VIDEO

Look into the future and learn about hydrogen fuel cell cars.

HANDS-ON LAB

Investigate Explore how the changing kinetic energy of a bouncing ball is related to conservation of energy.

Energy Is Conserved
Figure 5 After the ball is hit, it eventually slows down and falls. As it slows down, where does its kinetic energy go?

Energy Changes and the Law of Conservation

There is a certain amount of energy in the universe, and we cannot make more of it or destroy any that already exists. Another way to state this idea is to say that energy is conserved. When one object loses energy, other objects must gain it. This is known as the **law of conservation of energy**. This law is a factor in both energy transfers and energy transformations. Energy either moves from one place to another or changes forms, but no energy is created or destroyed.

When a baseball is hit by a bat, as in **Figure 5**, the ball flies through the air. The law of conservation of energy explains why it does not keep flying forever. The kinetic energy of the ball transfers to the air and transforms into thermal energy due to the force of friction. The more air particles there are, the more transfer there is. So more kinetic energy transfers to the air when the air is dense. That's why baseballs travel farther and faster at a baseball stadium in Denver, Colorado, where the air is thinner, than they do in low-altitude ballparks where the air is denser. You can learn more about this phenomenon in the Math Toolbox activity.

Conservation of Energy in Transfers Think back to the wrecking ball. Most of the kinetic energy in the moving ball is transferred directly to the wall. Any energy not transferred is transformed into thermal energy of the ball and air or the sound energy of the ball hitting the wall. Energy is conserved in this example, as it is in any example. No matter how energy is transformed or transferred, the total amount of energy in a system does not change.

Home Runs and Air Density

For more than 20 years, major league baseball games played in Denver, Colorado, have featured a high percentage of home runs. The high altitude of Denver means the air there is less dense than in lower-altitude locations, so balls flying through the air in Denver do not transfer as much energy to the air. They keep that kinetic energy and travel farther than they do in other ballparks. This table shows how many home runs the Colorado Rockies baseball team hit at home and away over 10 seasons.

Colorado Rockies's Home Runs at Home and Away										
	2007	2008	2009	2010	2011	2012	2013	2014	2015	2016
Home	103	92	98	108	94	100	88	119	102	116
Away	68	68	92	65	69	66	71	67	84	88

1. **SEP Use Mathematics** Over the 10-year span, how many more home runs did the Rockies score in their home ballpark in Denver than at other ballparks?

....

....

2. **Use Ratio Relationships** What is the ratio of home runs the team hit at home and home runs hit in away games over the 10-year period? Express the ratio in the smallest numbers possible.

....

....

3. **Summarize** Describe the high home-run numbers at the Rockies' home ball field in terms of kinetic energy and energy transformation.

....

....

....

....

....

....

....

....

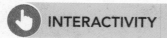

INTERACTIVITY

Explore the role that energy plays in extreme sports.

Conservation of Energy in Waves

The vibrations that come from a wrecking ball smashing through a wall travel in sound waves. In a sound wave or any other type of wave, energy passes through matter without moving the matter to a new place. The matter vibrates, meaning it moves temporarily, but ends up back where it was. We can see this on the ocean surface with a floating object (**Figure 6**). An ocean wave passes under the object, lifts it, drops it, and the object ends up back where it was. That's why a surfer cannot catch a wave far out in the ocean. Once a wave breaks, matter is moved and energy is released. A surfer can ride the wave when it breaks (**Figure 7**). Energy is conserved as the breaking wave transfers its energy to the shore.

☑ **READING CHECK** **Connect to Engineering** Why would the energy industry be interested in developing technologies to transform the kinetic energy in ocean waves to electrical energy?

Waves and Matter

Figure 6 A wave's energy passes through matter. Whether the medium is air, water, or some other substance, the matter vibrates but does not end up in a new place. Similarly, a floating ball moves in a circular motion as the wave passes, and the ball ends up back where it started.

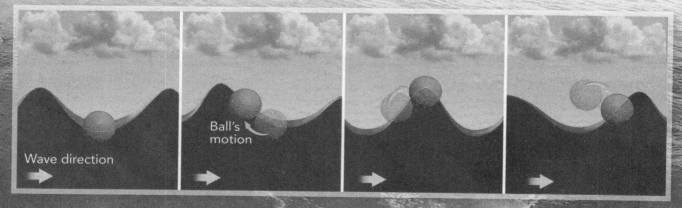

Wave direction

Ball's motion

Wave Energy

Figure 7 Ocean waves carry tremendous amounts of energy. When the wave breaks, the energy is released.

1. Distinguish Relationships What does it mean to say that energy is conserved in an energy transformation?

....

....

....

2. SEP Evaluate Information A train rumbles along the tracks at high speed. After it passes, the rail feels hot. What kind of energy transformation took place?

....

....

....

3. Connect to Society How are pendulums used in society? Give an example of a real-world pendulum that transfers a lot of energy.

....

....

....

4. SEP Construct Explanations Explain the changes in kinetic energy (KE) and potential energy (PE) that occur when an apple falls off the table and hits the floor.

....

....

....

....

....

....

5. SEP Engage in Argument After a tornado moves through a forest, what kinds of evidence would there be of energy transformations or transfers?

....

....

....

....

....

....

Quest CHECK-IN

In this lesson, you learned about energy transformations and energy transfers and how energy is conserved in both.

CCC Stability and Change Why is it important for engineers to understand and quantify how energy changes as it moves through a machine, or from one object to another?

....

....

....

....

HANDS-ON LAB

Redesign and Retest a Chain-Reaction Machine

Go online to download the lab worksheet. Modify your chain-reaction machine prototype to include at least one additional energy transformation. Then test, evaluate, and finalize the design, and present it to the class.

MS-PS3-5

U.S. ENERGY CONSUMPTION

As we know from the law of conservation of energy, new energy cannot simply be created. Therefore, many people feel that it's important for countries to study how they are using their energy resources. The pie chart shows the sources of energy used in the United States.

Renewable Energy

Light and heat from the sun, energy from wind and water, and heat from wood fires were the major sources of energy until the eighteenth century, when fossil fuels began to dominate. More recently, nations of the world have begun to return to renewable energy sources. These sources exist in an unlimited supply, and they are cleaner and safer for the environment. One disadvantage to renewable energy is the high initial cost involved in switching from fossil fuel systems to renewable energy systems.

Coal

Coal comes from the Earth, and it is easily transported. However, this fossil fuel must be mined from underground. The process damages the environment, and coal miners face some of the most dangerous work there is. Burning coal also releases pollutants into the atmosphere.

Petroleum

The main advantage to petroleum, also called crude oil, is that it is a powerful fuel. However, crude oil exists only in a limited supply. Petroleum also requires drilling to access it. The process is expensive and it damages the environment. Finally, the burning and accidental spilling of petroleum results in air pollution, land pollution, and water pollution on a vast scale.

Natural Gas

Natural gas is cheap and abundant. However, it must be transported through pipelines that often leak. Like petroleum, it requires drilling, which harms the environment. And burning natural gas releases carbon dioxide, which contributes to global warming.

Nuclear Energy

Nuclear energy is the most recently discovered source of power. It is a cleaner form of energy because it does not involve the burning of fossil fuels. The United States can generate its own nuclear power, so there are economic advantages as well. The major drawbacks to nuclear power are its expensive cost, the potential for accidents, and the need to dispose of radioactive wastes that will remain dangerous for thousands of years.

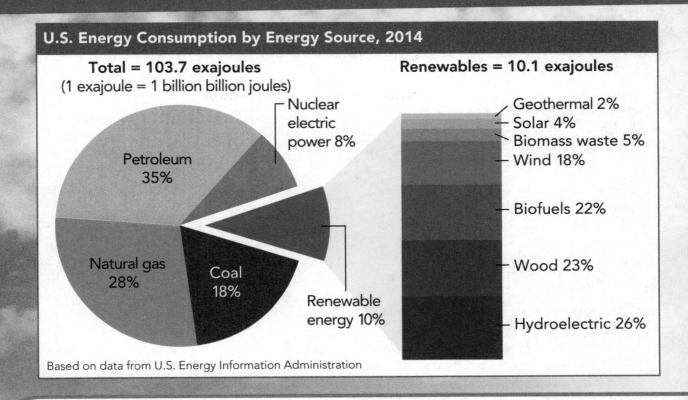

U.S. Energy Consumption by Energy Source, 2014

Total = 103.7 exajoules
(1 exajoule = 1 billion billion joules)

Petroleum 35%

Natural gas 28%

Coal 18%

Nuclear electric power 8%

Renewable energy 10%

Renewables = 10.1 exajoules

Geothermal 2%
Solar 4%
Biomass waste 5%
Wind 18%
Biofuels 22%
Wood 23%
Hydroelectric 26%

Based on data from U.S. Energy Information Administration

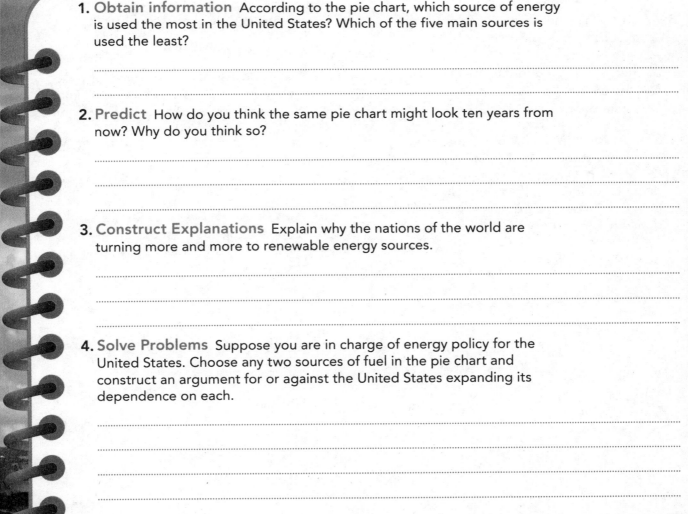

1. **Obtain information** According to the pie chart, which source of energy is used the most in the United States? Which of the five main sources is used the least?

....

....

2. **Predict** How do you think the same pie chart might look ten years from now? Why do you think so?

....

....

....

3. **Construct Explanations** Explain why the nations of the world are turning more and more to renewable energy sources.

....

....

....

4. **Solve Problems** Suppose you are in charge of energy policy for the United States. Choose any two sources of fuel in the pie chart and construct an argument for or against the United States expanding its dependence on each.

....

....

....

☑TOPIC 1 Review and Assess

1 Energy, Motion, Force, and Work

1. Which of the following is not a form of energy?
A. light
B. sound
C. air
D. electricity

2. How can you increase your power when stacking shoe boxes in a closet?
A. Spend more time stacking the boxes.
B. Stack fewer boxes per minute.
C. Slowly stack the boxes on a lower shelf.
D. Stack the boxes more quickly.

3. An object is in motion if
A. its position changes relative to its surroundings.
B. energy is applied to the object.
C. a force is applied to it.
D. it loses energy.

4. SEP Develop Models ✏ Draw a student carrying textbooks down a hallway. Label the drawing with arrows representing the direction of force on the textbooks and the direction of motion. Explain why no work is done on the textbooks as they are carried.

2 Kinetic Energy and Potential Energy

MS-PS3-1, MS-PS3-2

5. Kinetic energy is the energy of
A. motion.
B. potential.
C. gravity.
D. distance.

6. Which of the following is the best example of increasing an object's potential energy?
A. rolling a bowling ball
B. turning on a light bulb
C. stretching a rubber band
D. dropping a pencil

7. Gravitational potential energy is affected by the object's weight and the object's

....

8. SEP Use Mathematics A woman is walking at a rate of 0.5 m/s. Her mass is 62 kg. Calculate the woman's kinetic energy in joules.

....

....

....

9. Reason Quantitatively What has a greater effect on an object's kinetic energy—increasing its speed by 50 percent or increasing its mass by 75 percent? Explain.

....

....

....

....

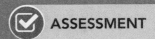

3 Other Forms of Energy

MS-PS3-5

10. In the process of fusion, nuclear energy is
   A. absorbed when a nucleus splits.
   B. released when a nucleus splits.
   C. released when nuclei join.
   D. absorbed when nuclei switch places.

11. Which of the following is a type of energy that is *not* involved in the human body's everyday processes?
   A. mechanical energy
   B. nuclear energy
   C. thermal energy
   D. chemical energy

12. An increase in the movement of particles in a substance is associated with an increase in .... energy.

13. Chemical energy is a form of .... energy.

14. SEP Construct Explanations A rubber ball that sits motionless near the edge of a tall bookshelf has no kinetic energy. However, it does have mechanical energy. Explain why this is possible.

....

....

....

....

....

4 Energy Change and Conservation

MS-PS3-5

15. Which of the following describes the law of conservation of energy?
   A. Energy cannot be created or destroyed.
   B. Energy can only be released through transformation.
   C. When energy is conserved, it always changes form.
   D. Energy increases when it is transferred from one object to another.

16. An energy ....
is the change of energy from one form to

another. An energy ....
is the movement of energy from one object to another.

17. 🖊 Draw a circle where the sled rider has the most potential energy. Draw a square where the rider has the most kinetic energy.

18. SEP Communicate Information Explain the energy transformation that must occur for your body to participate in a physical activity, such as playing a sport.

....

....

....

....

MS-PS3-2, MS-PS3-5

Evidence-Based Assessment

Darnell enters a design competition at school. The challenge is to construct a doorbell that works without electricity. The bell must ring loudly enough to be heard in another room of the house.

Darnell's idea is to use the bell, a ball, and gravity. A person would insert the ball into a hole in the wall. The ball would start from rest and fall a short distance to hit a bell. The ball would continue rolling back down and out to where the person could retrieve it in order to ring the bell again. Darnell draws a model of his doorbell design, as shown below.

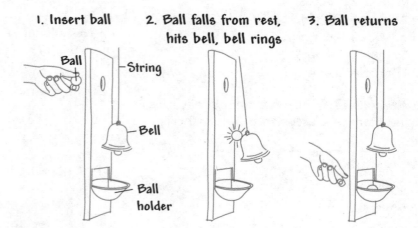

Darnell tests his design. For his first test, he uses a ping-pong ball, places the hole 1 meter above the ground, and hangs the bell 30 centimeters below the hole. He adds labels to his model to show how he set up his first test.

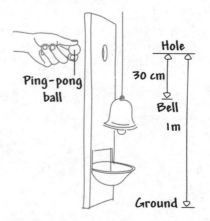

During this first test, Darnell finds that the bell does not ring loudly enough. Answer the following questions to help Darnell improve his design.

1. **CCC System Models** Which of the following two forms of energy are at play in Darnell's design?
   A. chemical energy and nuclear energy
   B. electromagnetic radiation and kinetic energy
   C. electrical energy and gravitational potential energy
   D. gravitational potential energy and kinetic energy

2. **SEP Defining Problems** Based on the results of his first test, Darnell needs to modify his design. What is the problem that Darnell needs to solve in his next doorbell test?

   ....

   ....

   ....

3. **SEP Construct Explanations** Describe the transformations and transfers of energy that are occurring in order for the bell to ring.

   ....

   ....

   ....

   ....

   ....

   ....

   ....

   ....

4. **SEP Construct Explanations** How could Darnell change his materials or design so that the bell rings more loudly? Provide two options, and explain how they work.

   ....

   ....

   ....

   ....

....

....

....

....

....

....

....

....

Quest FINDINGS

Complete the Quest!

Phenomenon Determine the best way to demonstrate your chain-reaction machine and show how energy is transformed and transferred from start to finish.

CCC Stability and Change How did energy change form as it made its way through your chain-reaction machine to perform a task?

....

....

....

....

....

....

....

....

....

....

👆 **INTERACTIVITY**

Reflect on Your Chain-Reaction Machine

MS-PS3-2, MS-PS3-5

3, 2, 1 . . . Liftoff!

Background

Phenomenon NASA is building a new website devoted to explaining the physics involved in launching rockets. They have asked you to help with a section of the website that deals with energy transfers and transformations. Your task is to design and build a model that explains the relationship between potential and kinetic energy in a rocket system.

> How can you **design** and build a **model** that explains the relationship between **potential and kinetic energy** in a rocket system?

Materials

(per group)

- scissors
- rubber bands
- meter stick
- marker
- metric ruler
- stapler
- cardboard tubes of varying diameters (from paper towels or wrapping paper)
- tape
- construction paper

Safety

Be sure to follow all safety guidelines provided by your teacher.

Design a Model

Demonstrate Go online for a downloadable worksheet of this lab.

☐ 1. Work with your group to develop a model of a rocket and launcher using the rubber bands, cardboard tubes, stapler, and other materials listed. Keep the following criteria in mind:

    A. Your rocket must be able to launch vertically into the air. As you work with your group, think about what each of the materials in your model will represent and how the model will operate.

    B. You will need to take at least three different measurements of how far the rubber band stretches and how far your rocket travels.

Plan Your Investigation

☐ 2. As a group, design an investigation to show that the amount of elastic potential energy in the rocket launcher system affects the kinetic energy of the rocket.

As you plan your investigation, consider these questions. Write your ideas in the space below.

- How can you use the meter stick and the ruler in your investigation?
- What tests will you perform?
- How many trials of each test will you perform?
- What variables will you measure?
- What are the dependent and independent variables?

....
....
....
....
....
....
....
....
....
....

☐ 3. After getting approval from your teacher for your model design and procedure, conduct your experiment. Record the data in your table. See if you can discover a relationship between how far the rubber band stretches and how far the rocket travels.

Sketch of Rocket Launcher Model

Procedure

....
....
....
....
....
....
....
....
....
....
....

Data Table

Distance Traveled by Rocket (cm)				
Rubber band stretch (cm)	Trial 1	Trial 2	Trial 3	Average

Analyze and Interpret Data

1. **Analyze Structures** Describe how your rocket launcher works. What might you do to improve it if you could do this experiment again?

   ....

   ....

   ....

   ....

2. **CCC Patterns** What is the relationship between the amount of potential energy in the rocket launcher system and the kinetic energy of the rocket? Explain.

   ....

   ....

   ....

   ....

3. **CCC Systems** What transfers of energy did you observe in the rocket launcher system? What transformation of energy did you observe? Remember to consider gravity in your answer.

   ....

   ....

   ....

   ....

4. **SEP Engage in Arguments** Use evidence from your investigation to support the argument that energy is being transferred and transformed throughout the rocket's travel. Draw a diagram that shows the rocket traveling upward, with different stages (on the ground, midway up, at its peak, and on its way down). Use labels to describe what is happening to the potential and kinetic energy at each stage. Label the position of maximum kinetic energy and the position of maximum potential energy.

TOPIC
2

Thermal Energy

LESSON 1
Thermal Energy, Heat, and Temperature
uInvestigate Lab: Temperature and Thermal Energy

LESSON 2
Heat Transfer
uInvestigate Lab: Visualizing Convection Currents

uEngineer It! **STEM** Shockwave to the Future

LESSON 3
Heat and Materials
uInvestigate Lab: Comparing How Liquids Cool

NGSS PERFORMANCE EXPECTATIONS

MS-PS3-3 Apply scientific principles to design, construct, and test a device that either minimizes or maximizes thermal energy transfer.

MS-PS3-4 Plan an investigation to determine the relationships among the energy transferred, the type of matter, the mass, and the change in the average kinetic energy of the particles as measured by the temperature of the sample.

MS-PS3-5 Construct, use, and present arguments to support the claim that when the kinetic energy of an object changes, energy is transferred to or from the object.

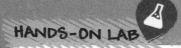

HANDS-ON LAB

uConnect See how well you can judge temperature differences.

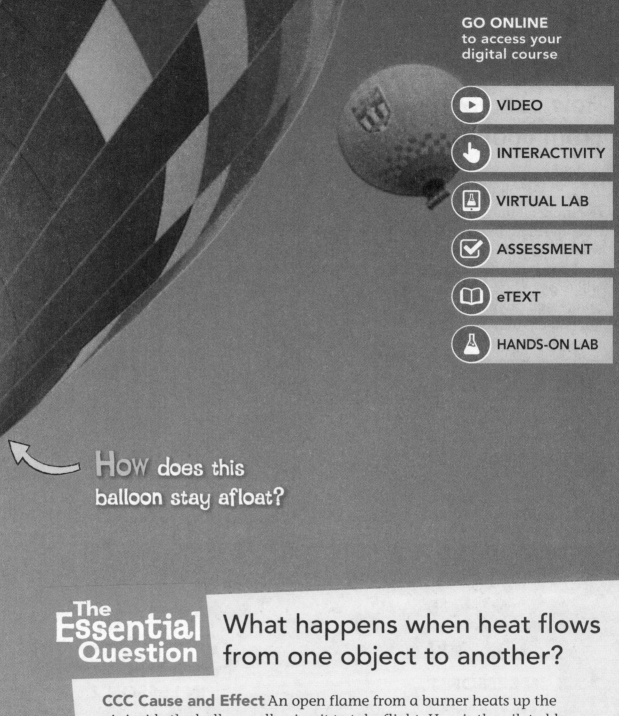

GO ONLINE
to access your
digital course

▶ VIDEO

👆 INTERACTIVITY

🧪 VIRTUAL LAB

☑ ASSESSMENT

📖 eTEXT

🧪 HANDS-ON LAB

How does this
balloon stay afloat?

The Essential Question

What happens when heat flows from one object to another?

CCC Cause and Effect An open flame from a burner heats up the air inside the balloon, allowing it to take flight. How is the pilot able to control the altitude of the balloon?

....

....

....

....

....

Quest KICKOFF

How can you keep hot water from cooling down?

STEM **Phenomenon** The Arctic is one of the harshest places on Earth. In the winter, researchers studying the Arctic climate face temperatures averaging –34°C (–30°F). In extremely cold places where it's important to stay warm, having the right gear can be a challenge. In this Quest activity, you will explore how heat is transferred between objects and design an insulating container that will keep hot liquids from cooling down quickly. As you work through the Quest, you will test and evaluate different materials. You will apply what you have learned to design and build a prototype of your container, testing and revising the design as necessary. Then you will reflect on the design process in the Findings activity.

NBC LEARN ▶ **VIDEO**

The Quest Kickoff video explores how humans—and even some animals—try to keep themselves warm by controlling the transfer of heat. After watching the video, write three questions you still have about how an insulating device helps limit the transfer of heat.

1
....
....

2
....
....

3
....
....

👆 **INTERACTIVITY**

Keep Hot Liquids Hot

MS-PS3-3 Apply scientific principles to design, construct, and test a device that either minimizes or maximizes thermal energy transfer.

IN LESSON 1
What happens to hot liquids when exposed to cold temperatures? Think about ways your insulating container can slow the flow of heat.

Quest CHECK-IN

IN LESSON 2
STEM How does heat transfer between objects? Consider how your insulating container must function. Then evaluate different materials you can use to build your container and design a solution.

 INTERACTIVITY

Contain the Heat

Researchers in the Arctic work in some of the coldest conditions on Earth.

Quest CHECK-INS

IN LESSON 3

STEM How can you apply what you know about thermal energy and heat transfer to build your container? Consider how different materials affect the flow of heat. Then build, test, and refine your design solution.

HANDS-ON LABS

- Keep the Heat In
- Keep the Cold Out

Quest FINDINGS

Complete the Quest!

Evaluate your work and reflect on the design and engineering process.

👆 INTERACTIVITY

Reflect on Your Insulating Container

How Cold Is the Water?

> How can you plan an investigation to **explain** whether you can use your senses to accurately determine temperature?

Background

Phenomenon The temperature of an object depends on the average kinetic energy of the particles that make up the object. Temperature can be measured with a thermometer, but how well does your hand work as a tool to judge temperature?

Materials

(per group)
- 3 large bowls
- warm tap water
- cold tap water
- room-temperature water
- markers
- thermometer
- paper

Safety

Be sure to follow all safety procedures provided by your teacher. The Safety Appendix of your textbook provides more details about the safety icons.

Design a Procedure

1. Fill one of the plastic bowls with cold water, another with warm water, and a third with water at room temperature. Label the bowls 1, 2, and 3 and line them up.

2. **SEP Plan a Procedure** Write a three-step procedure to make observations about the temperature of the water using your hands. Think about how you could "trick" your hands into perceiving the water at as cooler or warmer than it really is. Include a step that uses a thermometer. Show your plan to your teacher before you begin.

....

....

....

....

....

....

....

....

....

3. Record your observations in the table.

Observations

HANDS-ON LAB

Connect Go online for a downloadable worksheet of this lab.

Procedure Step	Observations

Analyze and Conclude

1. **SEP Interpret Data** How did the water in the bowls feel when you touched them at the start of the investigation?

....

....

2. **Explain Phenomena** Were you able to "trick" yourself into perceiving the water as cooler or warmer than it was when you began the investigation? Explain.

....

....

....

3. **SEP Construct an Explanation** Use your observations to explain if you can use hands to accurately judge temperature.

....

....

....

....

LESSON 1

Thermal Energy, Heat, and Temperature

Guiding Questions
- What happens to a substance when it is heated?
- What is the difference between thermal energy and temperature?

Connections
Literacy Use Information
Math Convert Measurement Units

MS-PS3-4

HANDS-ON LAB

uInvestigate Measure temperature change as energy is transferred.

Vocabulary
thermal energy
heat
temperature

Academic Vocabulary
transfer
absolute

Connect It!

✎ An ice pop will melt on a hot day. Circle the place on the ice pop where the particles have the most thermal energy.

Explain Phenomena Explain why you circled this place on the ice pop.

....

....

SEP Construct Explanations With enough time, would an ice pop melt on a cool autumn day? Explain.

....

....

Thermal Energy and Heat

All objects are made up of small particles. These particles are constantly in motion. This means they have kinetic energy. Particles are arranged in specific ways in different objects, so they also have potential energy. The total kinetic and potential energy of all the particles in an object is called **thermal energy**. This total energy can also be called internal energy. Objects contain thermal, or internal, energy even if they do not feel hot. The joule is the SI unit of energy.

The thermal energy of an object changes when heat is **transferred** to or from the object. **Heat** is the energy that is transferred from a warmer object to a cooler object. As the warmer object cools down, the cooler object warms up until the two objects are the same temperature. Once this happens, heat stops transferring between the two objects.

Heating a substance can cause its particles to move more quickly. For example, when the ice pop in **Figure 1** is held in sunlight, the particles in the ice pop gain kinetic energy. As a result, the temperature of the ice pop increases.

Note that in everyday language, the term *heat* can be used to describe the thermal energy contained in an object. However, when scientists use the term *heat*, they are referring only to energy that is transferred between two objects or systems at different temperatures.

✓READING CHECK **Compare and Contrast** What is the difference between thermal energy and heat?

....

....

INTERACTIVITY

See how heat flows with examples from the kitchen.

Academic Vocabulary

Heat is energy transferred from one place to another. What other things can you transfer from one place to another?

....

....

....

Thermal Energy Changes

Figure 1 An ice pop melts as its thermal energy increases. This thermal energy comes from heat radiated by the sun.

Academic Vocabulary

If something is absolute, it is definite or without question. How would you describe absolute silence?

....

....

....

....

Temperature And Its Measurement

We use temperature as a measure of how hot or cold something is. On average, the particles in a substance move faster when the substance is hot than when it is cold. **Temperature** is a measure of the average kinetic energy of the particles in a substance. When a substance is at a higher temperature, the particles move faster and have a greater average kinetic energy than when the substance is at a lower temperature.

Temperature can be measured with a thermometer. Thermometers show how hot or cold something is compared to a reference point. The Celsius scale uses the freezing point of water at sea level as its reference point at zero degrees Celsius (0°C). The United States typically uses the Fahrenheit scale, in which the freezing point of water at sea level is 32 degrees Fahrenheit (32°F). The kelvin is the official SI unit of temperature. On the Kelvin scale, zero kelvins (0 K) refers to **absolute** zero, the lowest temperature possible. At absolute zero, particles theoretically would have no kinetic energy. They would be completely motionless! So, the Kelvin scale only goes up from zero. Units on the Kelvin scale are the same size as units on the Celsius scale. A change of 1 K is the same temperature change as 1°C. Zero K is equal to −273°C.

Math Toolbox

Temperature Scales

If you have a thermometer with both Celsius and Fahrenheit scales, you can "eyeball" the conversion in temperature. Temperatures that line up on the parallel scales, such as 32°F and 0°C, are equivalent.

1. **Integrate with Visuals** 🖊 A comfortable room temperature is 72°F. Mark the thermometer where approximately 72°F would be. What is the approximate temperature in Celsius? ....

2. **Convert Measurement Units** 🖊 Complete the conversion table to compare the temperatures on different scales.

3. **SEP Use Mathematics** Write a formula for converting temperature to degrees Celsius if you are given the temperature in kelvins.

....

....

°F	°C	K
		263
	0	273
212	100	373

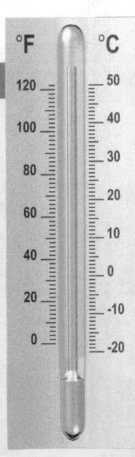

Figure 2 Icicles melt as their thermal energy increases. However, the temperature of the melting icicles remains at 0°C during the change of state.

CCC Stability and Change Think about the difference between thermal energy and temperature. How might the melting icicles gain energy without changing temperature?

....

....

....

....

How Thermal Energy and Temperature Are Related

Different objects at the same temperature can have different amounts of thermal energy. This is because the thermal energy of an object is the total energy of all the particles in the object. Temperature contributes to an object's thermal energy, but it is not the only factor. Other factors include the potential energy and arrangement of the particles, as well as the states, types, and amounts of matter in the object.

Changing States When thermal energy transfers to another object in the form of heat, it can do work or cause change like all other forms of energy. If enough heat is transferred to or from a substance, the substance can change states. During a change of state, the thermal energy of a substance changes, but its temperature stays the same. For example, as heat is transferred to the melting icicles in **Figure 2**, their thermal energy continues to increase. Since these icicles have already reached their melting point (0°C), the added energy continues to break the rigid arrangement of the water molecules, rather than increase their motion. This means that the average kinetic energy of the molecules themselves does not change during a change of state. Remember, temperature is a measure of the average kinetic energy of the molecules. Therefore, as the ice melts, the thermal energy of the ice increases while the temperature remains the same.

Literacy Connection

Use Information Use the text and an internet source to help you answer the following question: How does thermal energy relate to temperature during condensation?

....

....

....

....

Model It

Have you ever broken a piece of ice? You may have noticed that the break has angular edges instead of soft ones. This is because of the rigid, organized arrangement of its particles. The model shows the arrangement of water particles in a piece of solid ice just before it starts to melt.

 In the empty circle, draw what the particles would look like after the ice has begun melting. Then write a caption for your drawing that describes what it shows.

1. **CCC Energy and Matter** What is the temperature of the water in both images?

....

2. **Draw Comparative Inferences** Compare the relative amounts of thermal energy of each model.

....

....

....

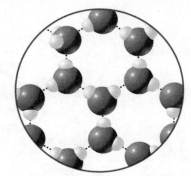

Water particles in solid form have a rigid arrangement.

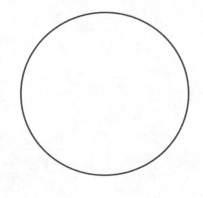

....

....

▶ VIDEO

Watch a video to help you understand changes of state.

Comparing Thermal Energy The amount of matter in an object affects its thermal energy. This is because more matter means more particles. As you have read, the particles have stored potential energy based on their arrangement. They also have kinetic energy based on their vibration and other movement. Therefore, the more particles an object has at a given temperature, the more thermal energy it has. For example, a 1-liter pot full of tea at 85°C has more thermal energy than a 0.2-liter cup full of tea at 85°C (**Figure 3**), because the pot contains more matter.

What if the objects contain the same amount of matter? The object at the higher temperature has more thermal energy. Remember, temperature is a measure of the average kinetic energy of the particles. If the object has a higher temperature, its particles have a greater average kinetic energy. A greater kinetic energy results in a greater thermal energy. So, if two 1-liter pots of tea have two different temperatures, the pot with the higher temperature has more thermal energy.

Thermal Energy and Amount of Matter

Figure 3 Even though the pot of tea and the cup of tea are at the same temperature, the pot of tea has more thermal energy because it contains more particles.

85°C

85°C

SEP Interpret Data If you wanted to cool both the pot and the cup of tea to 80°C, which one would take longer to cool down?

....

....

Changes in Temperature
What if we add the same amount of energy to the pot of tea and the cup of tea in **Figure 3**? Will they change to the same temperature? Not necessarily. An object's change in temperature depends on the environment and the types and amounts of matter in the object. Let's say we wanted to raise the temperature of the tea in each container by 1°C. The type of matter is the same, and the environment is the same. But the container with more tea will require more heat. It has more particles, so more energy is needed to get them all moving with the same average kinetic energy as the particles in the smaller cup of tea.

INTERACTIVITY

Discover how a thermometer works.

✓ **READING CHECK** **SEP Construct Explanations** Suppose you heat two bean burritos with the same ingredients in the microwave. One burrito weighs 0.3 pounds, while the other weighs 0.4 pounds. After microwaving each of them for one minute, which burrito will be hotter? Explain your answer.

....

....

....

Write About It Have you ever been served a meal that was not cooked hot enough? Write about the factors that may have contributed to your food being too cold.

MS-PS3-4

1. **SEP Communicating Information** What is the scientific definition of heat?

....

2. **Calculate** If the temperature outside is 297 K, what is this temperature in degrees Celsius?

....
....
....
....

3. **CCC Energy and Matter** What is the minimum value for the Kelvin temperature scale, and what would happen at that temperature?

....
....
....
....

4. **Identify** What are the factors that determine an object's thermal energy?

....
....
....

5. **Apply Concepts** Suppose that you have 0.5 liters of tomato soup and 0.5 liters of split pea soup in your kitchen. Can you tell for certain which one will require more thermal energy to heat up to 60°C? Why or why not?

....
....
....
....

6. **SEP Construct Explanations** Ice is melting at 0°C. Explain how the temperature of the melting ice stays the same while its thermal energy increases.

....
....
....
....
....

7. **Apply Scientific Reasoning** Object A has less thermal energy than Object B, but heat flows from Object A to Object B. What conditions would make this possible?

....
....
....
....

8. **CCC Cause and Effect** ✎ Jamie heats a pot of water on the stove. When the water boils, she turns the stove off and the water begins to cool. Draw a diagram with before and after pictures—before the stove is turned off, and after the stove is turned off. Add arrows to show the direction that heat flows in each picture.

MS-PS3-4

Glassblowing:
Not Just a Bunch of Hot Air

How do you think this colorful glass vase and bowl were made? It turns out that making something this beautiful is the result of heat transfer. Glass objects such as these are formed by a technique called glassblowing. This process involves using a very hot oven to soften the glass. A glassblower can then shape the glass because it is so pliable.

Consider the transfer of energy happening here. The heat from an oven or torch is transferred to the glass, causing the glass particles to move faster. As the particles move faster and faster, the glass softens. Once the glass is flexible, glassblowers blow air into it, forcing the glass to expand and change shape.

This glass blower heated solid glass until it became flexible. Now he shapes the blob of flexible glass into a new form.

CONNECT TO YOU

Heat transfers are happening all the time around you, whether you're cooking eggs for breakfast or using a hair dryer. Choose an example and develop a chart that shows where the heat transfers are and what change of state, if any, is occurring.

② Heat Transfer

Guiding Questions
- How is heat transferred?
- How is energy conserved during transformations?

Connections
Literacy Conduct Research Projects

Math Reason Quantitatively

MS-PS3-4, MS-PS3-5

HANDS-ON LAB

uInvestigate Observe convection currents with colored hot and cold water.

Vocabulary
conduction
convection
convection current
radiation

Academic Vocabulary
transform

Connect It!

✎ **When you're outside on a cold day, it's nice to stay warm near a fire. Draw an arrow on Figure 1 to show the direction of heat flow between the fire and the person's hands.**

Predict What happens in terms of heat transfer the longer you sit near the fire?

....

....

Infer Why would you rather have hot cocoa than lemonade on a cold day?

....

....

Types of Heat Transfer

Heat is transferring around you all the time. Heat doesn't transfer in random directions, though. It is transferred from warmer areas to cooler areas by conduction, convection, and radiation.

Conduction is the transfer of energy from one particle of matter to another within an object or between two objects that are in direct contact. Conduction occurs when you place your head on a cool pillow. The fast-moving particles in your skin collide with the slow-moving particles in the pillow. This causes the particles in the pillow to move faster. The pillow becomes warmer, while your skin becomes cooler.

Convection is a type of heat transfer that occurs through the movement of fluids, which can be solid, liquid, or gas. Fluids are materials that flow. When air is heated, its particles speed up and move farther apart. This makes the heated air less dense. The heated air rises to float on top of the denser, cooler air. Cooler air flows into its place, heats up, and rises. Previously heated air cools down, sinks, and the cycle repeats. This flow creates a circular motion known as a **convection current**. Convection currents in air cause wind and changes in the weather.

Radiation is the transfer of energy by electromagnetic waves. Radiation is the only form of heat transfer that does not require matter. You can feel the radiation from a fire without touching the flames, as in **Figure 1**. The sun's transfer of energy to Earth is another example of radiation. Sunlight travels 150 million kilometers through empty space before it warms Earth.

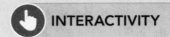

INTERACTIVITY

Watch this visual summary of conduction, convection, and radiation.

Warming Up
Figure 1 A fire feels especially warm to your hands on a cold day, when heat from your body quickly transfers to the frigid air.

Heat Flow

Figure 2 Heat transfer goes on all around you all the time.

✓ READING CHECK **Translate Information** ✏ In this lake scene, name each type of heat transfer shown and explain what it means. Then, draw arrows to show how heat is being transferred in each situation.

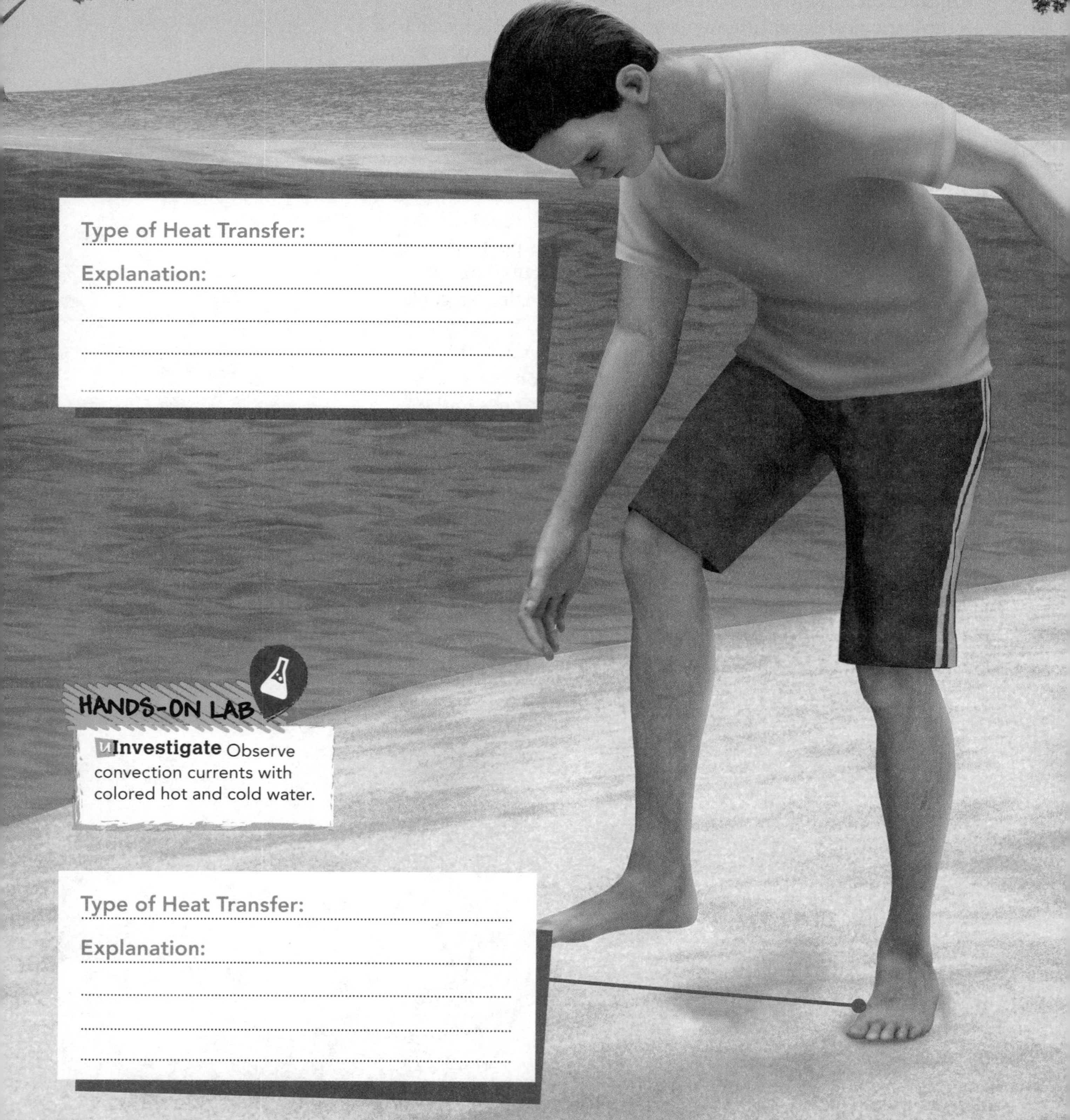

Type of Heat Transfer: ....

Explanation: ....

....

....

....

HANDS-ON LAB

✋**Investigate** Observe convection currents with colored hot and cold water.

Type of Heat Transfer: ....

Explanation: ....

....

....

....

Type of Heat Transfer: ....

Explanation: ....

....

....

Math Toolbox

Graphing Changes in Temperature

It's a hot day at the lake, with an air temperature of 30°C (86°F). Jeremy has two cups of water—one at 10°C and the other at 50°C. He places them on a picnic table where they receive the same amount of sunlight and no wind for a half an hour. The air temperature does not change during this time.

Cup 1

10°C

Cup 2

50°C

1. **Reason Quantitatively** ✎ Sketch two trend lines on the graph showing how the temperature of the water in the two cups would change over the 30 minutes. Create a legend to distinguish which line represents which cup (for example, the warmer cup = dotted line).

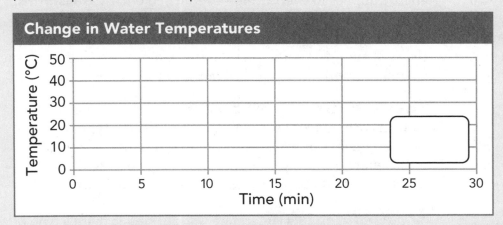

2. **SEP Construct Explanations** Describe the method(s) of heat transfer involved in causing the change in temperature of the two cups.

....

....

....

Heat Transfer

Figure 3 A wood-fired pizza oven demonstrates all three types of heat transfer: conduction, convection, and radiation.

SEP Construct Explanations ✏️
Draw arrows to show the direction of heat transfer. How is energy conserved in the system of the pizza and the wood-fired oven?

....
....
....
....
....

▶ **VIDEO**

See what it's like to become a firefighter.

Academic Vocabulary

What is another way of saying that energy can transform?

....
....
....

👆 **INTERACTIVITY**

Figure out the best method for reheating a pizza.

Energy Conservation

In conduction, convection, and radiation, energy is transferred from one place to another. Even though the energy moves, it is always conserved within a system. For instance, in the pizza oven shown in **Figure 3**, the oven loses energy, but the pizza gains that energy. So the total energy of the oven-pizza system is conserved. By the law of conservation of energy, energy cannot be created or destroyed.

Energy Transformations The law of conservation of energy applies to everything—even when energy **transforms**. Many energy transformations involve thermal energy. For example, an electric stove transforms electrical energy into thermal energy. Another kind of stove, a gas oven, converts the chemical energy from natural gas into thermal energy.

Thermal Energy and Work Thermal energy can be transformed to do work. For example, some types of train engines heat water to create steam. This causes pistons in the engine to move. The thermal energy of the water is transformed into the mechanical energy of the train.

✓ READING CHECK **Determine Conclusions** Is there a type of energy transformation in which the system destroys or creates energy? What conclusion can you draw?

....
....

Question It !

Alicia performed an experiment on squash soup. She wanted to see whether stirring the soup would really help it cool down faster. She heated two 10-ounce bowls of soup in a microwave for 120 seconds. Then, she stirred one bowl of soup with a spoon for 60 seconds and let the other sit for 60 seconds. She used two thermometers to make measurements, and she recorded her data in the chart below.

Temp of soup after heating (°F)	Stir or let sit for 60 seconds?	Temp after 60 seconds (°F)
150	Stir	137
150	Let sit	145

1. **SEP Construct Explanations** Describe the energy transformations involved in heating the soup in the microwave. Which method of heat transfer is involved in heating the soup?

....

....

....

....

....

....

....

....

2. **Summarize Data Sets** Based on the data, summarize Alicia's results. Describe how stirring the soup affects heat transfer.

....

....

....

....

....

....

....

....

....

....

....

....

Literacy Connection

Conduct Research Projects Perform the experiment, and think about what you've learned about heat transfer in this lesson. Then, write a new question that would explore these concepts further. Discuss the possible answers to your question with a partner or teacher.

....

....

....

Write About It Think about how your breakfast or lunch was prepared. How did thermal energy come into play?

MS-PS3-4, MS-PS3-5

1. **Classify** What type of heat transfer occurs when eggs fry in a hot pan?

....

2. **Identify** What type of heat transfer occurs when you roast a marshmallow by holding it over a campfire?

....

3. **CCC Energy and Matter** Name a type of food in which convection helps the cooking process. Explain your answer.

....

....

....

4. **Explain Phenomena** When you touch a warm picnic table, your hand becomes warmer. Explain how energy conservation applies to this situation.

....

....

....

....

5. **SEP Develop Models** ✏ Draw a picture that shows a convection current in a real-life situation. Use arrows to represent the convection current.

6. **SEP Construct Explanations** Give a real-world example of how energy is transformed from electrical energy to thermal energy. Describe how the heat can be transferred to other objects through conduction, convection, or radiation.

....

....

....

....

Quest CHECK-IN

So far, you have learned how energy can be transferred by means of conduction, convection, and radiation.

SEP Define Problems Why is it important to consider the types of materials that are available and how those materials interact with cold exterior temperatures and warm interior temperatures of a food container?

....

....

....

....

👆 INTERACTIVITY

Contain the Heat

Go online to apply what you've learned about thermal energy and heat transfer. How can you use this knowledge to design your insulating container? Brainstorm possible solutions with a group, and record your work in a graphic organizer. Then select the best method and materials to use in your design.

SHOCKWAVE TO THE FUTURE

▶ VIDEO

See how engineers use energy transformations to develop a real-world solution.

How do you make car engines more efficient? You engineer them! The new shockwave engine offers a better way to get where you are going.

The Challenge: To build a more efficient engine.

Phenomenon Most cars on the road today still contain combustion engines. These engines use pistons to run. The pistons make the car heavier, and they also cause friction that wastes energy.

The shockwave engine does not contain pistons. It is more like a fan, circular in shape and ringed with blades. The shockwave engine converts the chemical energy of fuel into heat, and pressure increases within the engine. The thermal energy is converted to mechanical energy when the blades begin to spin. These spinning blades cause a crankshaft to turn, which causes the wheels of the car to spin.

The shockwave engine has fewer moving parts, and it is lighter than combustion engines. It can improve fuel economy by about 60 percent!

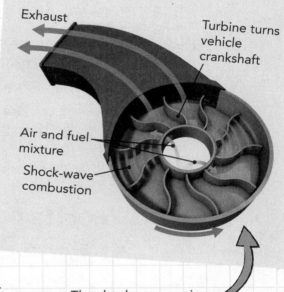

Exhaust

Turbine turns vehicle crankshaft

Air and fuel mixture

Shock-wave combustion

The shockwave engine works with thermal energy and pressure, causing a simple spinning motion. No pistons required!

DESIGN CHALLENGE

How can you build a simple heat engine? Go to the Engineering Design Notebook to find out!

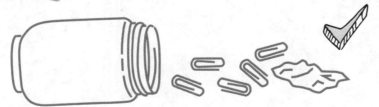

Case Study

Earth Power

Electricity is the largest form of energy used in the United States. Power plants generate this energy using a variety of sources. These sources include fossil fuels (such as natural gas and coal), nuclear power, hydroelectric, wind, and solar.

Coal used to be the major source of electricity, but it is one of the most expensive sources. It is also harmful to human health and the environment. Many coal plants, which produce soot and toxic gases, are now changing to natural gas, which is cheaper and cleaner. The burning of all fossil fuels releases carbon dioxide, which is a greenhouse gas that affects the climate.

Geothermal energy can also be used to generate electricity. In this process, warm water deep underground is pumped to the surface. The thermal energy of the water is transformed into electricity within a power plant. Review the steps in the diagram.

How a Geothermal POWER PLANT Works

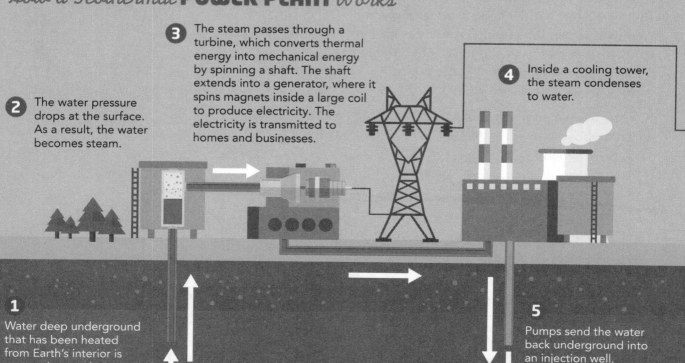

3 The steam passes through a turbine, which converts thermal energy into mechanical energy by spinning a shaft. The shaft extends into a generator, where it spins magnets inside a large coil to produce electricity. The electricity is transmitted to homes and businesses.

4 Inside a cooling tower, the steam condenses to water.

2 The water pressure drops at the surface. As a result, the water becomes steam.

1 Water deep underground that has been heated from Earth's interior is pumped up to the surface.

5 Pumps send the water back underground into an injection well.

Geothermal on the Rise

Over the past 10 years, the demand for geothermal energy has increased greatly. While it is still one of the less common ways to generate electricity, it is a much cleaner method than burning coal, and it has garnered public support. A disadvantage to using geothermal energy is that it is very expensive to generate and transmit, and the number of sites where geothermal energy is accessible from Earth's surface is not as high as the number of sites where natural gas, oil, and coal can be found. Still, there are significant efforts to increase demand for renewable energy resources, such as geothermal, solar, and wind, to reduce our impact on the environment.

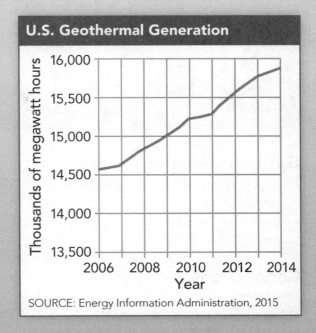

U.S. Geothermal Generation

SOURCE: Energy Information Administration, 2015

Use the graph to answer the following questions.

1. **Patterns** Describe any patterns you see in the graph.

   ....

   ....

2. **Predict** What do you think the data will look like for the generation of geothermal energy through the year 2040 in the United States? Why?

   ....

   ....

3. **Construct Explanations** The country of Iceland resides in a very volcanically active location. Geothermal plants provide 25 percent of Iceland's electricity. What factors do you think contribute to the high percentage of energy supplied by geothermal sources in Iceland?

   ....

   ....

4. **Communicate** What do you think could be done to encourage more people to use geothermal energy?

   ....

   ....

   ....

Heat and Materials

Guiding Questions

• How do different materials respond to heat?

• How is friction related to thermal energy and temperature?

Connections

Literacy Integrate with Visuals

Math Analyze Proportional Relationships

MS-PS3-4, MS-PS3-5

HANDS-ON LAB

uInvestigate Explore how different amounts of liquid change temperature.

Vocabulary

conductor
insulator
specific heat
thermal
 expansion

Academic Vocabulary

contract

Connect It !

🖋 **When divers explore deep ocean waters, the temperatures they encounter are very cold. In the space provided, describe how you think the wetsuit keeps the diver warm in cold water.**

Communicate You also use special clothing to stay warm and perform different functions. What items of clothing do you use for specific activities?

....

....

Relate Structure and Function What materials are those items made of?

....

Thermal Properties of Materials

When you bake something in the oven, you use dishes made of glass, ceramic, or metal instead of plastic. Some materials can stand up to the heat of an oven better than others. Materials respond to heat in different ways. The thermal properties of an object determine how it will respond to heat.

Conductors and Insulators If you walk barefoot from your living room rug to the tile floor of your kitchen, you will notice that the tile feels colder than the rug. But the temperature of the rug and the tile are the same—room temperature! The difference has to do with how materials conduct heat, which is another way of saying how well they absorb or transmit heat.

A material that conducts heat well is called a **conductor**. Metals such as silver are good conductors. Some materials are good conductors because of the particles they contain and how those particles are arranged. A good conductor, such as the tile floor, feels cold to the touch because heat easily transfers out of your skin and into the tile. However, heat also transfers out of conductors easily. A metal flagpole feels much hotter on a summer day than a wooden pole would in the same place because heat easily conducts out of the metal pole and into your hand.

A wooden pole and your living room rug are good insulators. **Insulators** are materials that do not conduct heat well. Other good insulators include air and wool. For example, wool blankets slow the transfer of heat out of your body.

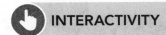
INTERACTIVITY

Determine what kind of container to use when taking lunch to the beach.

Reflect Conductors and insulators are all around you. In your science notebook, write one conductor and one insulator that you see. Describe their materials and why you believe they are conductors or insulators.

Surviving the Cold Water
Figure 1 A diver stays warm in a special wetsuit.

HANDS-ON LAB

Investigate Explore how different amounts of liquid change temperature.

VIRTUAL LAB

Explore energy changes with a calorimeter and investigate the amount of calories in different foods.

Specific Heat Imagine running across hot sand toward the ocean. You run to the water's edge, but you don't go any farther— the water is too cold. How can the sand be so hot and the water so cold? After all, the sun heats both of them. The answer is that water requires more heat to raise its temperature than sand does.

When a substance or material is heated, its temperature rises. But the temperature does not rise at the same rate for all materials. The amount of heat required to raise the temperature of a material depends on the material's chemical makeup. Different materials require different amounts of energy to have the same temperature increase.

The amount of energy required to raise the temperature of 1 kilogram of a material by 1 kelvin is called its **specific heat**. It is measured in joules per kilogram-kelvin, or J/(kg·K), where kelvin is a measure of temperature. A material with a high specific heat can absorb a great deal of energy without a great change in temperature.

If a material's temperature changes, you can calculate how its energy changes with a formula.

Energy Change = Mass × Specific Heat × Temperature Change

Math Toolbox

Energy Change, Specific Heat, and Mass

A chef is preparing vegetables in two pans. The pans are the same mass, but one is made of aluminum and the other is made of iron. She heats both pans to the same temperature before adding the vegetables.

1. **Analyze Proportional Relationships** The ratio of the specific heat of aluminum to the specific heat of iron is 2:1. How much energy must be transferred to the aluminum pan, compared with the amount of energy transferred to the iron pan?

....

....

2. **CCC Energy and Matter** If the chef used an aluminum pan and a silver pan of equal mass, which would undergo a greater energy change?

....

....

Material	Specific Heat (J/(kg·K))
Aluminum	900
Water	4,180
Silver	235
Iron	450

3. **Predict** Suppose the chef used two silver pans instead, but one was three times the mass of the other. How would the energy change of the two pans compare?

....

....

Pop!

Figure 2 When you make popcorn, heat flows to a tiny droplet of water inside the kernel. This causes the liquid water to change into vapor. The expanding water vapor builds up pressure inside the kernel. Finally, the kernel explodes, turning into a piece of popcorn!

Thermal Expansion Have you ever tried to open a jar, but the lid was firmly stuck? Thermal expansion could help you in this situation. To loosen a jar lid, you can hold it under a stream of hot water. This works because the metal lid expands more than the glass does as it gets hotter.

As the thermal energy of matter increases, its particles usually spread out, causing the substance to expand. This is true for almost all types of matter. The expansion of matter when it is heated is known as **thermal expansion**. When matter is cooled, the opposite happens. Thermal energy is released. This causes the particles to slow down and move closer together. As matter cools, it usually decreases in volume, or **contracts**. Different materials expand and contract at different rates and to different volumes.

Academic Vocabulary

In this context, the verb *contract* means to decrease in size. Write a sentence using the word *contract*.

....

....

Expansion Joints

Figure 3 Bridge joints allow room for the bridge to expand in the heat.

✓ **READING CHECK** **Write Informative Texts**
What might happen if thermal expansion had not been considered in the building of this bridge?

....

....

....

....

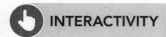
Temperature, Energy, and Friction

The kinetic energy of particles can change, as in thermal expansion, but an entire object's kinetic energy can change as well. A change in an object's kinetic energy indicates that a transfer of energy to or from the object is happening. If the kinetic energy of the object increases, then some form of energy is being transferred to the object. If the kinetic energy decreases, then the object is transferring kinetic energy to something else. This is true because energy is always conserved. The kinetic energy is not created or destroyed—it is transferred and sometimes transformed to other forms of energy in the process.

Friction and Energy Transformation

Some objects lose kinetic energy because of friction. The law of conservation of energy accounts for this change in energy. For example, when a bike skids to a stop, as in **Figure 4**, the tires experience friction with the ground. When this happens, the kinetic energy of the entire bike changes—the bike slows down. Where does that kinetic energy go? If you could feel the bike tire or the ground, you would observe the answer. They both become hot. As friction slows the bike, the kinetic energy transforms into thermal energy of the tire and the ground. As the tire and the ground cool down, that thermal energy transfers to the surrounding air.

From Fast to Warm
Figure 4 As this bike skids to a stop, the tires and the ground become warmer.

Literacy Connection

Integrate With Visuals
How does friction between the bike tires and the ground relate to thermal energy and temperature?

....
....
....
....

Model It!

Friction and Energy Transformation
In the space provided, draw an example in which friction causes kinetic energy to transfer and transform. Describe the transfers or transformations that are occurring.

....
....
....

Space Shuttle Entering Atmosphere
Figure 5 This NASA illustration shows how a space shuttle burns through the atmosphere as it returns to Earth.

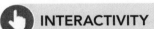

Materials for Space Shuttles When space shuttles were used for various missions, friction occurred between the space shuttles and the air in Earth's atmosphere. When a shuttle returned from space and re-entered the atmosphere, as in **Figure 5**, it experienced compression and friction from the atmospheric gas. Even though the upper atmosphere is cold, the space shuttle experienced high temperatures due to friction. Some of the kinetic energy of the moving space shuttle transformed into thermal energy.

Space shuttles were built with materials that can withstand both the high temperatures when moving through the atmosphere and the cold temperatures of outer space. Scientists developed Ultra High Temperature Ceramics for the front end of space shuttles. These materials withstood extremely high temperatures. A space shuttle also had a layer of insulating material below its outer layer. The insulation layer prevented the heat from transferring into the interior of the shuttle. It also prevented heat from transferring out of the shuttle's interior once the shuttle entered the cold of outer space.

INTERACTIVITY

Evaluate and recommend materials in the design of a playhouse for a park.

☑ READING CHECK **Infer** Which type of material, an insulator or a conductor, should be used to keep an airplane warm inside? Why?

....

....

Materials for Airplanes

Figure 6 Various materials including titanium, graphite-epoxy, and wood have have been used to construct airplanes. Use the information in the table to help you answer the questions.

Material	Advantages	Disadvantages
Wood	Lightweight, strong	Splinters, requires maintenance
Aluminum	Lightweight, strong	Cannot withstand temperatures at high speeds
Steel	Stronger than aluminum, stiff	heavy
Graphite-epoxy	Lighter than aluminum, strong, thin sheets can be stacked	Not as strong as steel
Titanium	As strong as steel, lightweight	expensive

1. **Claim** Which material do you think would be best for the outside of a high-speed airplane?

....

2. **Evidence**   Use the information in the table to construct an argument for your choice.

....

....

....

3. **Reasoning** What additional information would you like to know to ensure that it is suitable for the outside of the aircraft?

....

....

....

MS-PS3-4, MS-PS3-5

1. SEP Construct Explanations Why do some materials feel hotter than others, even if the two materials are at the same temperature?

....

....

....

....

....

2. Classify Foam picnic coolers keep food cool on a hot day. Is foam a conductor or an insulator? Explain.

....

....

....

3. Calculate Suppose you have two slices of cheese. They have the same specific heat, but one is twice the mass of the other. How much energy is needed to melt the larger slice compared to the amount of energy needed to melt the smaller slice?

....

....

4. SEP Communicate Information Why do objects tend to expand when they are heated?

....

....

....

....

....

....

....

5. SEP Engage in Argument The driver of a car slams on the brakes so that his car does not crash into a deer in the road. What happens to the thermal energy of the tires as the car skids to a stop? What causes this change in thermal energy?

....

....

....

....

....

....

Quest CHECK-INS

In this lesson, you learned how the specific heat of different substances affects how they transfer heat and whether they're likely to be classified as insulators or conductors.

Evaluate How could the specific heat of the substance your container will hold affect the performance of the container?

....

....

....

HANDS-ON LABS

- Keep the Heat In
- Keep the Cold Out

Go online to download the lab worksheets. You will finalize the design of your container, and then build, test, and evaluate the finished product.

☑ TOPIC 2 Review and Assess

1 Thermal Energy, Heat, and Temperature

MS-PS3-4

1. What is the total energy of all of the particles in an object called?
   A. chemical energy
   B. thermal energy
   C. potential energy
   D. nuclear energy

2. Energy that is transferred from a warmer object to a cooler object is called
   A. temperature.
   B. substance.
   C. heat.
   D. mechanical energy.

3. When the kinetic energy of the particles in an object increases, the temperature of the object
   A. increases.
   B. decreases.
   C. remains the same.
   D. becomes fixed at 100°C.

4. A/an _____ is an instrument that can be used to measure temperature.

5. CCC Stability and Change What happens to the state of liquid water if enough heat is added?

....

....

6. Draw Comparative Inferences A 2-ounce apple and a 4-ounce apple are at the same temperature. Which requires more thermal energy to raise its temperature by 1°F? Why?

....

....

....

....

Use the illustration to answer questions 7 and 8.

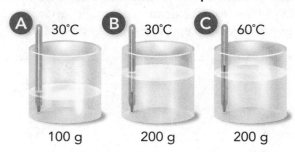

7. SEP Interpret Data Compare the average motion of the particles in the three containers of water. Explain your answer. (Note: The same substance is in each container.)

....

....

....

....

8. SEP Analyze Data Compare the amount of thermal energy in containers A and B. Explain your answer.

....

....

....

2 Heat Transfer

MS-PS3-4, MS-PS3-5

9. What is the process by which heat transfers from one particle of matter to another when the particles collide?
   A. conduction   B. convection
   C. expansion   D. radiation

10. When energy transforms from one form to another, the total amount of energy in the system
   A. decreases.   B. increases.
   C. is conserved.   D. drops to zero.

11. Air currents transfer energy by the method of heat transfer called ....

12. Identify each example of heat transfer as conduction, convection, or radiation.

A.

B.

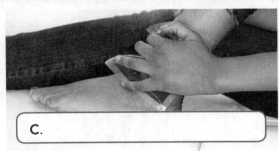

C.

13. Explain How can heat be transferred across empty space? Explain your answer.

....

....

14. Make Judgments Suppose you try to heat up your home using a fireplace in one of the rooms. Would a fan be helpful? Explain.

....

....

....

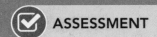
3 Heat and Materials

MS-PS3-4, MS-PS3-5

15. Which kinds of materials do not conduct heat well?
   A. insulators
   B. conductors
   C. metals
   D. radiators

16. The amount of energy per kilogram needed to increase the temperature of a material by 1 K is called the
   A. specific heat.
   B. heat sensitivity.
   C. heat resistance.
   D. thermal heat.

17. The speeds of two bumper cars decrease as their bumpers rub against each other. What happens to the temperatures of the bumpers due to the force of friction?
   A. Both bumpers cool down.
   B. Both bumpers warm up.
   C. One bumper cools down while the other warms up.
   D. Both bumpers remain the same temperature.

18. SEP Develop Models 🖊 Draw before and after diagrams of the particles in a log that is heated. Does the log expand or contract?

MS-PS3-4, MS-PS3-5

Evidence-Based Assessment

Out in space, sand-sized particles of rock approach Earth every single day. However, they do not reach Earth's surface because they burn up in the atmosphere. Sometimes, larger space rocks called meteoroids also travel through the atmosphere. Once the meteoroid enters the atmosphere, it appears as a bright light moving through the sky, called a meteor. A meteoroid typically enters the atmosphere with an average speed in the range of 10–70 km/s. The rock burns as it travels, losing mass and speed in the process. The burning is due to friction between the meteoroid and the air particles in the atmosphere. The density of the air particles in the atmosphere is greater closer to Earth's surface. Some meteoroids do not burn up completely, and they reach Earth's surface as meteorites.

The following data provides information about three meteoroids traveling towards Earth's surface. The meteoroids are all roughly spherical and of the same density.

Meteoroid	Initial Mass (kg)	Surface temperature of meteoroid in space, before entering atmosphere (°C)	Surface temperature of meteoroid in atmosphere, 150 km above Earth's surface (°C)
1	0.52	90	1730
2	3.24	92	1727
3	1.05	91	1735

1. **CCC Cause and Effect** Which statement describes what happens to the kinetic energy of the particles in the atmosphere as they come into contact with the meteoroid?

   A. The kinetic energy of the surrounding air particles is converted to electrical energy.

   B. The average kinetic energy of the surrounding air particles increases.

   C. The kinetic energy of the surrounding air particles is converted to potential energy.

   D. The average kinetic energy of the surrounding air particles decreases.

2. **Cite Evidence** What happens to the kinetic energy of a meteoroid as it travels farther through the atmosphere toward Earth's surface? Support your claim with evidence from the information provided.

   ....
   ....
   ....
   ....
   ....
   ....
   ....
   ....

3. **Infer** Explain how two methods of heat transfer are involved as the meteoroid burns.

   ....
   ....
   ....
   ....
   ....
   ....
   ....
   ....
   ....

4. **SEP Construct Explanations** Which meteoroid is most likely to reach Earth's surface? Explain why this is so, in terms of heat transfer. Use data from the table to support your response.

   ....
   ....
   ....
   ....
   ....
   ....
   ....

Quest FINDINGS

Complete the Quest!

Phenomenon After applying what you learned to the design and construction of an insulating container, reflect on the use of models and scientific principles in the design of your containers.

SEP Design Solutions How did concepts related to thermal energy and heat transfer guide your design process?

....
....
....
....
....
....

INTERACTIVITY

Reflect on Your Insulating Container

83

Testing Thermal Conductivity

How can you **design** an experiment to determine the best **metal** to use for a **heat sink**?

Background

Phenomenon Electronics manufacturers use heat sinks to draw heat away from components that can overheat. Engineers for a new tablet company have designed a super-fast processor. The problem is, the processor gets very hot, causing the tablet to shut down. The company has asked you to design an experiment to provide evidence for the best metal to use for a heat sink in their new tablet.

Materials

(per group)

- 3 metal conducting strips (10 cm x 2 cm each): copper, aluminum, and brass
- 6 insulating foam cups (5 cm tall)
- aluminum foil
- 2 plastic-backed thermometers
- boiling water (75 mL)
- room-temperature water (40 mL)
- graduated cylinder
- scissors
- stopwatch

Safety

Be sure to follow all safety procedures provided by your teacher. Appendix B of your textbook provides additional details about the safety icons.

heat sink

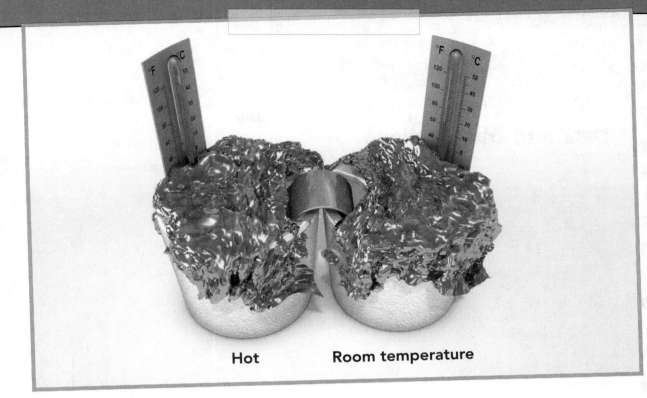

Hot   Room temperature

Develop Possible Solutions

HANDS-ON LAB

⬇ **Demonstrate** Go online for a downloadable worksheet of this lab.

⬜ ⚠ You will conduct an experiment to investigate how each of the three metals conducts heat from a cup of hot water to a cup of room-temperature water. Design an experiment using the materials provided. Write out a procedure below, and then conduct the experiment. Construct a data table to record the results of your experiment, and note any important observations you make.

....

....

....

....

....

....

....

....

....

....

....

....

....

....

Data and Observations

Analyze and Interpret Data

1. **Apply Scientific Reasoning** What roles did the metal strips and the foam cups play in terms of heat transfer?

   ....

   ....

   ....

   ....

2. **SEP Use Mathematics** Determine the temperature change of the room temperature water after 10 minutes for each metal used.

   Copper: ....

   Aluminum: ....

   Brass: ....

3. **SEP Use Mathematics** Determine the average rate of temperature change of the room temperature water for each metal used.

   Copper: ....

   Aluminum: ....

   Brass: ....

4. **SEP Engage in Argument** Brass costs about $0.90 per pound, copper costs $2.15 per pound, and aluminum costs $0.75 per pound. Which metal would you recommend be used for for use as a heat sink in the tablet? Explain your choice.

   ....

   ....

   ....

5. **Provide Critique** Examine the setup and procedure for another group's experiment. Make recommendations to the group for improving the design of its experiment.

   ....

   ....

   ....

   ....

SEP.1, SEP.8

The Meaning of Science

Science Skills

Reflect Think about a time you misplaced something and could not find it. Write a sentence defining the problem. What science skills could you use to solve the problem? Explain how you would use at least three of the skills in the table.

Science is a way of learning about the natural world. It involves asking questions, making predictions, and collecting information to see if the answer is right or wrong.

The table lists some of the skills that scientists use. You use some of these skills every day. For example, you may observe and evaluate your lunch options before choosing what to eat.

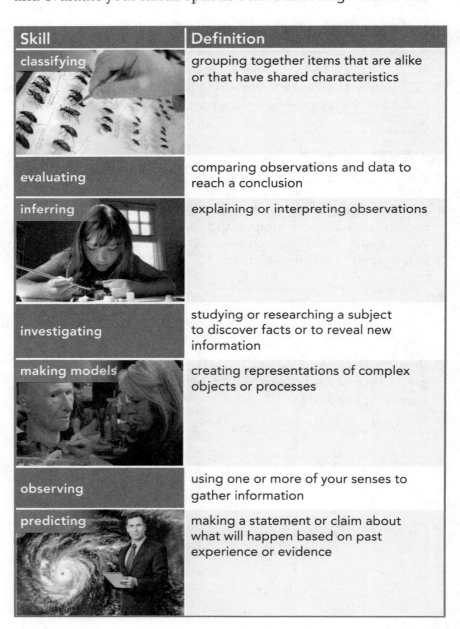

Skill	Definition
classifying	grouping together items that are alike or that have shared characteristics
evaluating	comparing observations and data to reach a conclusion
inferring	explaining or interpreting observations
investigating	studying or researching a subject to discover facts or to reveal new information
making models	creating representations of complex objects or processes
observing	using one or more of your senses to gather information
predicting	making a statement or claim about what will happen based on past experience or evidence

Scientific Attitudes

Curiosity often drives scientists to learn about the world around them. Creativity is useful for coming up with inventive ways to solve problems. Such qualities and attitudes, and the ability to keep an open mind, are essential for scientists.

When sharing results or findings, honesty and ethics are also essential. Ethics refers to rules for knowing right from wrong.

Being skeptical is also important. This means having doubts about things based on past experiences and evidence. Skepticism helps to prevent accepting data and results that may not be true.

Scientists must also avoid bias—likes or dislikes of people, ideas, or things. They must avoid experimental bias, which is a mistake that may make an experiment's preferred outcome more likely.

Scientific Reasoning

Scientific reasoning depends on being logical and objective. When you are objective, you use evidence and apply logic to draw conclusions. Being subjective means basing conclusions on personal feelings, biases, or opinions. Subjective reasoning can interfere with science and skew results. Objective reasoning helps scientists use observations to reach conclusions about the natural world.

Scientists use two types of objective reasoning: deductive and inductive. Deductive reasoning involves starting with a general idea or theory and applying it to a situation. For example, the theory of plate tectonics indicates that earthquakes happen mostly where tectonic plates meet. You could then draw the conclusion, or deduce, that California has many earthquakes because tectonic plates meet there.

In inductive reasoning, you make a generalization from a specific observation. When scientists collect data in an experiment and draw a conclusion based on that data, they use inductive reasoning. For example, if fertilizer causes one set of plants to grow faster than another, you might infer that the fertilizer promotes plant growth.

Make Meaning
Think about a bias the marine biologist in the photo could show that results in paying more or less attention to one kind of organism over others. Make a prediction about how that bias could affect the biologist's survey of the coral reef.

Write About It
Suppose it is raining when you go to sleep one night. When you wake up the next morning, you observe frozen puddles on the ground and icicles on tree branches. Use scientific reasoning to draw a conclusion about the air temperature outside. Support your conclusion using deductive or inductive reasoning.

SEP.1, SEP.2, SEP.3, SEP.4, CCC.4

Science Processes

Scientific Inquiry

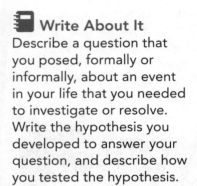
Scientists contribute to scientific knowledge by conducting investigations and drawing conclusions. The process often begins with an observation that leads to a question, which is then followed by the development of a hypothesis. This is known as scientific inquiry.

One of the first steps in scientific inquiry is asking questions. However, it's important to make a question specific with a narrow focus so the investigation will not be too broad. A biologist may want to know all there is to know about wolves, for example. But a good, focused question for a specific inquiry might be "How many offspring does the average female wolf produce in her lifetime?"

A hypothesis is a possible answer to a scientific question. A hypothesis must be testable. For something to be testable, researchers must be able to carry out an investigation and gather evidence that will either support or disprove the hypothesis.

Scientific Models

Models are tools that scientists use to study phenomena indirectly. A model is any representation of an object or process. Illustrations, dioramas, globes, diagrams, computer programs, and mathematical equations are all examples of scientific models. For example, a diagram of Earth's crust and mantle can help you to picture layers deep below the surface and understand events such as volcanic eruptions.

Models also allow scientists to represent objects that are either very large, such as our solar system, or very small, such as a molecule of DNA. Models can also represent processes that occur over a long period of time, such as the changes that have occurred throughout Earth's history.

Models are helpful, but they have limitations. Physical models are not made of the same materials as the objects they represent. Most models of complex objects or processes show only major parts, stages, or relationships. Many details are left out. Therefore, you may not be able to learn as much from models as you would through direct observation.

Reflect Identify the benefits and limitations of using a plastic model of DNA, as shown here.

Science Experiments

An experiment or investigation must be well planned to produce valid results. In planning an experiment, you must identify the independent and dependent variables. You must also do as much as possible to remove the effects of other variables. A controlled experiment is one in which you test only one variable at a time.

For example, suppose you plan a controlled experiment to learn how the type of material affects the speed at which sound waves travel through it. The only variable that should change is the type of material. This way, if the speed of sound changes, you know that it is a result of a change in the material, not another variable such as the thickness of the material or the type of sound used.

You should also remove bias from any investigation. You may inadvertently introduce bias by selecting subjects you like and avoiding those you don't like. Scientists often conduct investigations by taking random samples to avoid ending up with biased results.

Once you plan your investigation and begin to collect data, it's important to record and organize the data. You may wish to use a graph to display and help you to interpret the data.

Communicating is the sharing of ideas and results with others through writing and speaking. Communicating data and conclusions is a central part of science.

Scientists share knowledge, including new findings, theories, and techniques for collecting data. Conferences, journals, and websites help scientists to communicate with each other. Popular media, including newspapers, magazines, and social media sites, help scientists to share their knowledge with nonscientists. However, before the results of investigations are shared and published, other scientists should review the experiment for possible sources of error, such as bias and unsupported conclusions.

Write About It
List four ways you could communicate the results of a scientific study about the health of sea turtles in the Pacific Ocean.

SEP.1, SEP.6, SEP.7, SEP.8

Scientific Knowledge

Scientific Explanations

Suppose you learn that adult flamingos are pink because of the food they eat. This statement is a scientific explanation—it describes how something in nature works or explains why it happens. Scientists from different fields use methods such as researching information, designing experiments, and making models to form scientific explanations. Scientific explanations often result from many years of work and multiple investigations conducted by many scientists.

Scientific Theories and Laws

A scientific law is a statement that describes what you can expect to occur every time under a particular set of conditions. A scientific law describes an observed pattern in nature, but it does not attempt to explain it. For example, the law of superposition describes what you can expect to find in terms of the ages of layers of rock. Geologists use this observed pattern to determine the relative ages of sedimentary rock layers. But the law does not explain why the pattern occurs.

By contrast, a scientific theory is a well-tested explanation for a wide range of observations or experimental results. It provides details and describes causes of observed patterns. Something is elevated to a theory only when there is a large body of evidence that supports it. However, a scientific theory can be changed or overturned when new evidence is found.

Write About It
Choose two fields of science that interest you. Describe a method used to develop scientific explanations in each field.

SEP Construct Explanations Complete the table to compare and contrast a scientific theory and a scientific law.

	Scientific Theory	Scientific Law
Definition		
Does it attempt to explain a pattern observed in nature?		

Analyzing Scientific Explanations

To analyze scientific explanations that you hear on the news or read in a book such as this one, you need scientific literacy. Scientific literacy means understanding scientific terms and principles well enough to ask questions, evaluate information, and make decisions. Scientific reasoning gives you a process to apply. This includes looking for bias and errors in the research, evaluating data, and identifying faulty reasoning. For example, by evaluating how a survey was conducted, you may find a serious flaw in the researchers' methods.

Evidence and Opinions

The basis for scientific explanations is empirical evidence. Empirical evidence includes the data and observations that have been collected through scientific processes. Satellite images, photos, and maps of mountains and volcanoes are all examples of empirical evidence that support a scientific explanation about Earth's tectonic plates. Scientists look for patterns when they analyze this evidence. For example, they might see a pattern that mountains and volcanoes often occur near tectonic plate boundaries.

To evaluate scientific information, you must first distinguish between evidence and opinion. In science, evidence includes objective observations and conclusions that have been repeated. Evidence may or may not support a scientific claim. An opinion is a subjective idea that is formed from evidence, but it cannot be confirmed by evidence.

Write About It
Suppose the conservation committee of a town wants to gauge residents' opinions about a proposal to stock the local ponds with fish every spring. The committee pays for a survey to appear on a web site that is popular with people who like to fish. The results of the survey show 78 people in favor of the proposal and two against it. Do you think the survey's results are valid? Explain.

Make Meaning
Explain what empirical evidence the photograph reveals.

SEP.3, SEP.4

Tools of Science

Measurement

Making measurements using standard units is important in all fields of science. This allows scientists to repeat and reproduce other experiments, as well as to understand the precise meaning of the results of others. Scientists use a measurement system called the International System of Units, or SI.

For each type of measurement, there is a series of units that are greater or less than each other. The unit a scientist uses depends on what is being measured. For example, a geophysicist tracking the movements of tectonic plates may use centimeters, as plates tend to move small amounts each year. Meanwhile, a marine biologist might measure the movement of migrating bluefin tuna on the scale of kilometers.

Units for length, mass, volume, and density are based on powers of ten—a meter is equal to 100 centimeters or 1000 millimeters. Units of time do not follow that pattern. There are 60 seconds in a minute, 60 minutes in an hour, and 24 hours in a day. These units are based on patterns that humans perceived in nature. Units of temperature are based on scales that are set according to observations of nature. For example, 0°C is the temperature at which pure water freezes, and 100°C is the temperature at which it boils.

Write About It

Suppose you are planning an investigation in which you must measure the dimensions of several small mineral samples that fit in your hand. Which metric unit or units will you most likely use? Explain your answer.

Measurement	Metric units
Length or distance	meter (m), kilometer (km), centimeter (cm), millimeter (mm) 1 km = 1,000 m 1 cm = 10 mm 1 m = 100 cm
Mass	kilogram (kg), gram (g), milligram (mg) 1 kg = 1,000 g 1 g = 1,000 mg
Volume	cubic meter (m^3), cubic centimeter (cm^3) 1 m^3 = 1,000,000 cm^3
Density	kilogram per cubic meter (kg/m^3), gram per cubic centimeter (g/cm^3) 1,000 kg/m^3 = 1 g/cm^3
Temperature	degrees Celsius (°C), kelvin (K) 1°C = 273 K
Time	hour (h), minute (m), second (s)

Math Skills

Using numbers to collect and interpret data involves math skills that are essential in science. For example, you use math skills when you estimate the number of birds in an entire forest after counting the actual number of birds in ten trees.

Scientists evaluate measurements and estimates for their precision and accuracy. In science, an accurate measurement is very close to the actual value. Precise measurements are very close, or nearly equal, to each other. Reliable measurements are both accurate and precise. An imprecise value may be a sign of an error in data collection. This kind of anomalous data may be excluded to avoid skewing the data and harming the investigation.

Other math skills include performing specific calculations, such as finding the mean, or average, value in a data set. The mean can be calculated by adding up all of the values in the data set and then dividing that sum by the number of values.

Hour	Number of Ducks Observed at a Pond
1	12
2	10
3	2
4	14
5	13
6	10
7	11

SEP Use Mathematics The data table shows how many ducks were seen at a pond every hour over the course of seven hours. Is there a data point that seems anomalous? If so, cross out that data point. Then, calculate the mean number of ducks on the pond. Round the mean to the nearest whole number.

Graphs

Graphs help scientists to interpret data by helping them to find trends or patterns in the data. A line graph displays data that show how one variable (the dependent or outcome variable) changes in response to another (the independent or test variable). The slope and shape of a graph line can reveal patterns and help scientists to make predictions. For example, line graphs can help you to spot patterns of change over time.

Scientists use bar graphs to compare data across categories or subjects that may not affect each other. The heights of the bars make it easy to compare those quantities. A circle graph, also known as a pie chart, shows the proportions of different parts of a whole.

Write About It
You and a friend record the distance you travel every 15 minutes on a one-hour bike trip. Your friend wants to display the data as a circle graph. Explain whether or not this is the best type of graph to display your data. If not, suggest another graph to use.

SEP.1, SEP.2, SEP.3, SEP.6

The Engineering Design Process

Engineers are builders and problem solvers. Chemical engineers experiment with new fuels made from algae. Civil engineers design roadways and bridges. Bioengineers develop medical devices and prosthetics. The common trait among engineers is an ability to identify problems and design solutions to solve them. Engineers use a creative process that relies on scientific methods to help guide them from a concept or idea all the way to the final product.

Define the Problem

To identify or define a problem, different questions need to be asked: *What are the effects of the problem? What are the likely causes? What other factors could be involved?* Sometimes the obvious, immediate cause of a problem may be the result of another problem that may not be immediately apparent. For example, climate change results in different weather patterns, which in turn can affect organisms that live in certain habitats. So engineers must be aware of all the possible effects of potential solutions. Engineers must also take into account how well different solutions deal with the different causes of the problem.

Reflect Write about a problem that you encountered in your life that had both immediate, obvious causes as well as less-obvious and less-immediate ones.

As engineers consider problems and design solutions, they must identify and categorize the criteria and constraints of the project.

Criteria are the factors that must be met or accomplished by the solution. For example, a gardener who wants to protect outdoor plants from deer and rabbits may say that the criteria for the solution are "plants are no longer eaten" and "plant growth is not inhibited in any way." The gardener then knows the plants cannot simply be sealed off from the environment, because the plants will not receive sunlight and water.

The same gardener will likely have constraints on his solution, such as budget for materials and time that is available for working on the project. By setting constraints, a solution can be designed that will be successful without introducing a new set of problems. No one wants to spend $500 on materials to protect $100 worth of tomatoes and cucumbers.

Develop Possible Solutions

After the problem has been identified, and the criteria and constraints identified, an engineer will consider possible solutions. This often involves working in teams with other engineers and designers to brainstorm ideas and research materials that can be used in the design.

It's important for engineers to think creatively and explore all potential solutions. If you wanted to design a bicycle that was safer and easier to ride than a traditional bicycle, then you would want more than just one or two solutions. Having multiple ideas to choose from increases the likelihood that you will develop a solution that meets the criteria and constraints. In addition, different ideas that result from brainstorming can often lead to new and better solutions to an existing problem.

Make Meaning
Using the example of a garden that is vulnerable to wild animals such as deer, make a list of likely constraints on an engineering solution to the problem you identified before. Determine if there are common traits among the constraints, and identify categories for them.

Design a Solution

Engineers then develop the idea that they feel best solves the problem. Once a solution has been chosen, engineers and designers get to work building a model or prototype of the solution. A model may involve sketching on paper or using computer software to construct a model of the solution. A prototype is a working model of the solution.

Building a model or prototype helps an engineer determine whether a solution meets the criteria and stays within the constraints. During this stage of the process, engineers must often deal with new problems and make any necessary adjustments to the model or prototype.

Test and Evaluate a Solution

Whether testing a model or a prototype, engineers use scientific processes to evaluate their solutions. Multiple experiments, tests, or trials are conducted, data are evaluated, and results and analyses are communicated. New criteria or constraints may emerge as a result of testing. In most cases, a solution will require some refinement or revision, even if it has been through successful testing. Refining a solution is necessary if there are new constraints, such as less money or available materials. Additional testing may be done to ensure that a solution satisfies local, state, or federal laws or standards.

Make Meaning Think about an aluminum beverage can. What would happen if the price or availability of aluminum changed so much that cans needed to be made of a new material? What would the criteria and constraints be on the development of a new can?

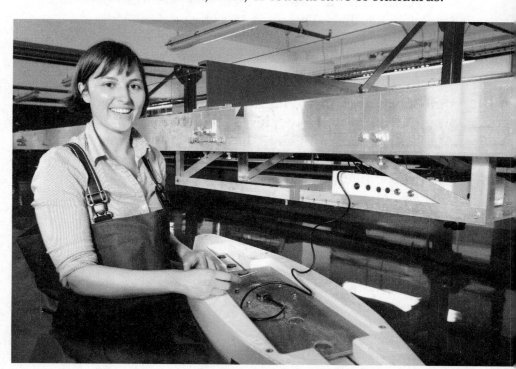

A naval architect sets up a model to test how the the hull's design responds to waves.

Communicate the Solution

Engineers need to communicate the final design to the people who will manufacture the product. This may include sketches, detailed drawings, computer simulations, and written text. Engineers often provide evidence that was collected during the testing stage. This evidence may include graphs and data tables that support the decisions made for the final design.

If there is feedback about the solution, then the engineers and designers must further refine the solution. This might involve making minor adjustments to the design, or it might mean bigger modifications to the design based on new criteria or constraints. Any changes in the design will require additional testing to make sure that the changes work as intended.

Redesign and Retest the Solution

At different steps in the engineering and design process, a solution usually must be revised and retested. Many designs fail to work perfectly, even after models and prototypes are built, tested, and evaluated. Engineers must be ready to analyze new results and deal with any new problems that arise. Troubleshooting, or fixing design problems, allows engineers to adjust the design to improve on how well the solution meets the need.

SEP Communicate Information Suppose you are an engineer at an aerospace company. Your team is designing a rover to be used on a future NASA space mission. A family member doesn't understand why so much of your team's time is taken up with testing and retesting the rover design. What are three things you would tell your relative to explain why testing and retesting are so important to the engineering and design process?

Safety Symbols

These symbols warn of possible dangers in the laboratory and remind you to work carefully.

 Safety Goggles Wear safety goggles to protect your eyes in any activity involving chemicals, flames or heating, or glassware.

 Lab Apron Wear a laboratory apron to protect your skin and clothing from damage.

 Breakage Handle breakable materials, such as glassware, with care. Do not touch broken glassware.

 Heat-Resistant Gloves Use an oven mitt or other hand protection when handling hot materials, such as hot plates or hot glassware.

 Plastic Gloves Wear disposable plastic gloves when working with harmful chemicals and organisms. Keep your hands away from your face, and dispose of the gloves according to your teacher's instructions.

 Heating Use a clamp or tongs to pick up hot glassware. Do not touch hot objects with your bare hands.

 Flames Before you work with flames, tie back loose hair and clothing. Follow your teacher's instructions about lighting and extinguishing flames.

 No Flames When using flammable materials, make sure there are no flames, sparks, or other exposed heat sources present.

 Corrosive Chemical Avoid getting acid or other corrosive chemicals on your skin or clothing or in your eyes. Do not inhale the vapors. Wash your hands after the activity.

 Poison Do not let any poisonous chemical come into contact with your skin, and do not inhale its vapors. Wash your hands when you are finished with the activity.

 Fumes Work in a well-ventilated area when harmful vapors may be involved. Avoid inhaling vapors directly. Test an odor only when directed to do so by your teacher, and use a wafting motion to direct the vapor toward your nose.

 Sharp Object Scissors, scalpels, knives, needles, pins, and tacks can cut your skin. Always direct a sharp edge or point away from yourself and others.

 Animal Safety Treat live or preserved animals or animal parts with care to avoid harming the animals or yourself. Wash your hands when you are finished with the activity.

 Plant Safety Handle plants only as directed by your teacher. If you are allergic to certain plants, tell your teacher; do not do an activity involving those plants. Avoid touching harmful plants such as poison ivy. Wash your hands when you are finished with the activity.

 Electric Shock To avoid electric shock, never use electrical equipment around water, when the equipment is wet, or when your hands are wet. Be sure cords are untangled and cannot trip anyone. Unplug equipment not in use.

 Physical Safety When an experiment involves physical activity, avoid injuring yourself or others. Alert your teacher if there is any reason you should not participate.

 Disposal Dispose of chemicals and other laboratory materials safely. Follow the instructions from your teacher.

 Hand Washing Wash your hands thoroughly when finished with an activity. Use soap and warm water. Rinse well.

 General Safety Awareness When this symbol appears, follow the instructions provided. When you are asked to develop your own procedure in a lab, have your teacher approve your plan.

Using a Laboratory Balance

The laboratory balance is an important tool in scientific investigations. Different kinds of balances are used in the laboratory to determine the masses and weights of objects. You can use a triple-beam balance to determine the masses of materials that you study or experiment with in the laboratory. An electronic balance, unlike a triple-beam balance, is used to measure the weights of materials.

The triple-beam balance that you may use in your science class is probably similar to the balance depicted in this Appendix. To use the balance properly, you should learn the name, location, and function of each part of the balance.

Triple-Beam Balance

The triple-beam balance is a single-pan balance with three beams calibrated in grams. The back, or 100-gram, beam is divided into ten units of 10 grams each. The middle, or 500-gram, beam is divided into five units of 100 grams each. The front, or 10-gram, beam is divided into ten units of 1 gram each. Each gram on the front beam is further divided into units of 0.1 gram.

Apply Concepts What is the greatest mass you could find with the triple-beam balance in the picture?

....

Calculate What is the mass of the apple in the picture?

....

The following procedure can be used to find the mass of an object with a triple-beam balance:

1. Place the object on the pan.

2. Move the rider on the middle beam notch by notch until the horizontal pointer on the right drops below zero. Move the rider back one notch.

3. Move the rider on the back beam notch by notch until the pointer again drops below zero. Move the rider back one notch.

4. Slowly slide the rider along the front beam until the pointer stops at the zero point.

5. The mass of the object is equal to the sum of the readings on the three beams.

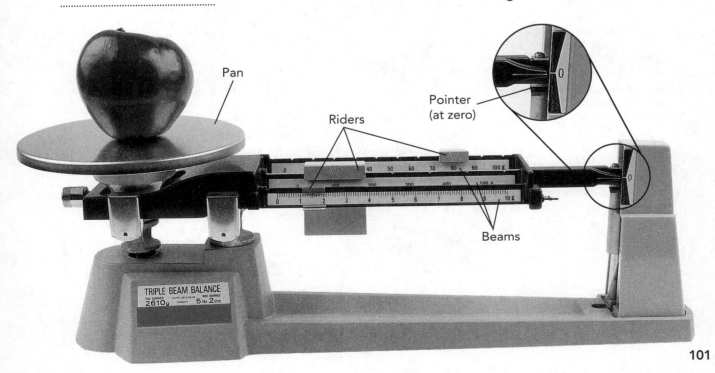

Pan

Riders

Pointer (at zero)

Beams

TRIPLE BEAM BALANCE
700 SERIES   800 SERIES
2610 g   CAPACITY 5 lb 2 oz

Using a Microscope

The microscope is an essential tool in the study of life science. It allows you to see things that are too small to be seen with the unaided eye.

You will probably use a compound microscope like the one you see here. The compound microscope has more than one lens that magnifies the object you view.

Typically, a compound microscope has one lens in the eyepiece (the part you look through). The eyepiece lens usually magnifies 10×. Any object you view through this lens will appear 10 times larger than it is.

A compound microscope may contain two or three other lenses called objective lenses. They are called the low-power and high-power objective lenses. The low-power objective lens usually magnifies 10×. The high-power objective lenses usually magnify 40× and 100×.

To calculate the total magnification with which you are viewing an object, multiply the magnification of the eyepiece lens by the magnification of the objective lens you are using. For example, the eyepiece's magnification of 10× multiplied by the low-power objective's magnification of 10× equals a total magnification of 100×.

Use the photo of the compound microscope to become familiar with the parts of the microscope and their functions.

The Parts of a Microscope

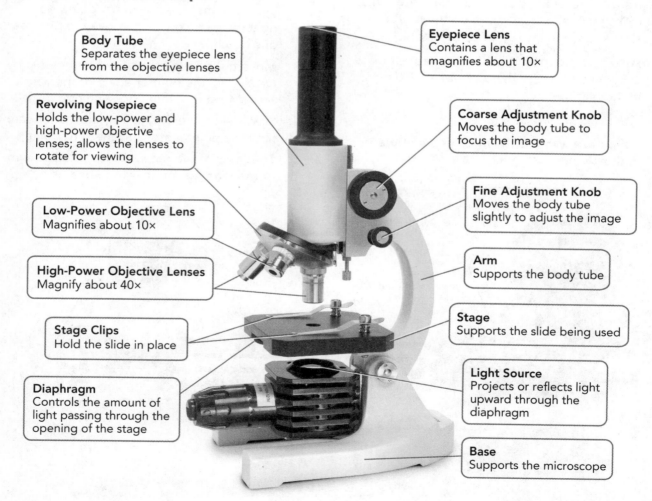

Body Tube
Separates the eyepiece lens from the objective lenses

Eyepiece Lens
Contains a lens that magnifies about 10×

Revolving Nosepiece
Holds the low-power and high-power objective lenses; allows the lenses to rotate for viewing

Coarse Adjustment Knob
Moves the body tube to focus the image

Low-Power Objective Lens
Magnifies about 10×

Fine Adjustment Knob
Moves the body tube slightly to adjust the image

High-Power Objective Lenses
Magnify about 40×

Arm
Supports the body tube

Stage Clips
Hold the slide in place

Stage
Supports the slide being used

Diaphragm
Controls the amount of light passing through the opening of the stage

Light Source
Projects or reflects light upward through the diaphragm

Base
Supports the microscope

Using the Microscope

Use the following procedures when you are working with a microscope.

1. To carry the microscope, grasp the microscope's arm with one hand. Place your other hand under the base.

2. Place the microscope on a table with the arm toward you.

3. Turn the coarse adjustment knob to raise the body tube.

4. Revolve the nosepiece until the low-power objective lens clicks into place.

5. Adjust the diaphragm. While looking through the eyepiece, adjust the mirror until you see a bright white circle of light. **CAUTION:** Never use direct sunlight as a light source.

6. Place a slide on the stage. Center the specimen over the opening on the stage. Use the stage clips to hold the slide in place. **CAUTION:** Glass slides are fragile.

7. Look at the stage from the side. Carefully turn the coarse adjustment knob to lower the body tube until the low-power objective almost touches the slide.

8. Looking through the eyepiece, very slowly turn the coarse adjustment knob until the specimen comes into focus.

9. To switch to the high-power objective lens, look at the microscope from the side. Carefully revolve the nosepiece until the high-power objective lens clicks into place. Make sure the lens does not hit the slide.

10. Looking through the eyepiece, turn the fine adjustment knob until the specimen comes into focus.

Making a Wet-Mount Slide

Use the following procedures to make a wet-mount slide of a specimen.

1. Obtain a clean microscope slide and a coverslip. **CAUTION:** Glass slides and coverslips are fragile.

2. Place the specimen on the center of the slide. The specimen must be thin enough for light to pass through it.

3. Using a plastic dropper, place a drop of water on the specimen.

4. Gently place one edge of the coverslip against the slide so that it touches the edge of the water drop at a 45° angle. Slowly lower the coverslip over the specimen. If you see air bubbles trapped beneath the coverslip, tap the coverslip gently with the eraser end of a pencil.

5. Remove any excess water at the edge of the coverslip with a paper towel.

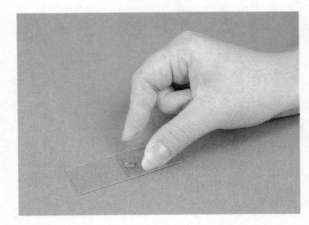

Periodic Table of Elements

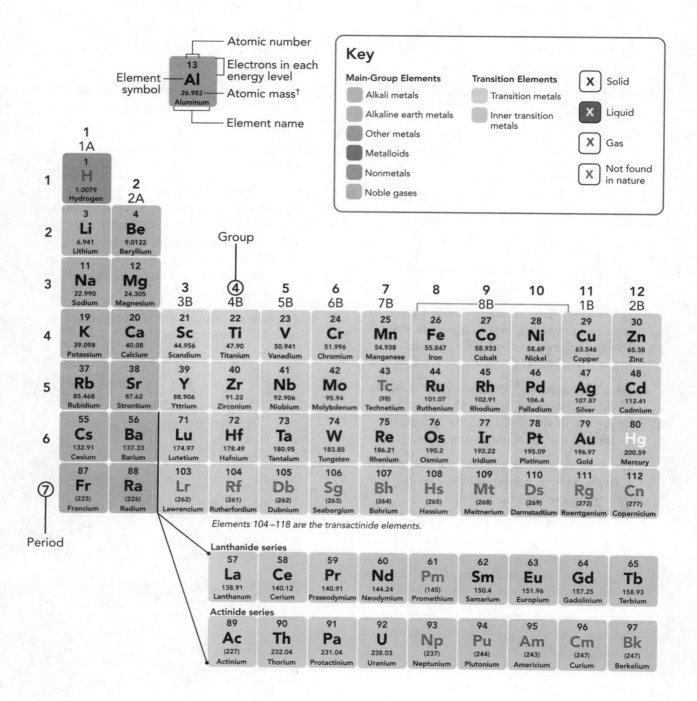

†The atomic masses in parentheses are the mass numbers of the longest-lived isotope of elements for which a standard atomic mass cannot be defined.

13 3A	14 4A	15 5A	16 6A	17 7A	18 8A
					2 **He** 4.0026 Helium
5 **B** 10.81 Boron	6 **C** 12.011 Carbon	7 **N** 14.007 Nitrogen	8 **O** 15.999 Oxygen	9 **F** 18.998 Fluorine	10 **Ne** 20.179 Neon
13 **Al** 26.982 Aluminum	14 **Si** 28.086 Silicon	15 **P** 30.974 Phosphorus	16 **S** 32.06 Sulfur	17 **Cl** 35.453 Chlorine	18 **Ar** 39.948 Argon
31 **Ga** 69.72 Gallium	32 **Ge** 72.59 Germanium	33 **As** 74.922 Arsenic	34 **Se** 78.96 Selenium	35 **Br** 79.904 Bromine	36 **Kr** 83.80 Krypton
49 **In** 114.82 Indium	50 **Sn** 118.69 Tin	51 **Sb** 121.75 Antimony	52 **Te** 127.60 Tellurium	53 **I** 126.90 Iodine	54 **Xe** 131.30 Xenon
81 **Tl** 204.37 Thallium	82 **Pb** 207.2 Lead	83 **Bi** 208.98 Bismuth	84 **Po** (209) Polonium	85 **At** (210) Astatine	86 **Rn** (222) Radon
113 **Nh** (284) Nihonium	114 **Fl** (289) Flerovium	115 **Mc** (288) Moscovium	116 **Lv** (292) Livermorium	117 **Ts** (294) Tennessine	118 **Og** (294) Oganesson

66 **Dy** 162.50 Dysprosium	67 **Ho** 164.93 Holmium	68 **Er** 167.26 Erbium	69 **Tm** 168.93 Thulium	70 **Yb** 173.04 Ytterbium
98 **Cf** (251) Californium	99 **Es** (252) Einsteinium	100 **Fm** (257) Fermium	101 **Md** (258) Mendelevium	102 **No** (259) Nobelium

GLOSSARY

C

chemical energy A form of potential energy that is stored in chemical bonds between atoms. (26)

conduction The transfer of thermal energy from one particle of matter to another. (63)

conductor A material that conducts heat well. (73)

convection The transfer of thermal energy by the movement of a fluid. (63)

convection current The movement of a fluid, caused by differences in temperature, that transfers heat from one part of the fluid to another. (63)

E

elastic potential energy The energy of stretched or compressed objects. (19)

electrical energy The energy of electric charges. (27)

electromagnetic radiation The energy transferred through space by electromagnetic waves. (27)

energy The ability to do work or cause change. (5)

F

force A push or pull exerted on an object. (6)

G

gravitational potential energy Potential energy that depends on the height of an object. (18)

H

heat The transfer of thermal energy from a warmer object to a cooler object. (55)

I

insulator A material that does not conduct heat well. (73)

K

kinetic energy Energy that an object has due to its motion. (15)

L

law of conservation of energy The rule that energy cannot be created or destroyed. (36)

M

mechanical energy Kinetic or potential energy associated with the motion or position of an object. (23)

medium The material through which a wave travels. (27)

motion The state in which one object's distance from another is changing. (5)

N

nuclear energy The potential energy stored in the nucleus of an atom. (24)

P

potential energy The energy an object has because of its position; also the internal stored energy of an object, such as energy stored in chemical bonds. (17)

power The rate at which one form of energy is transformed into another. (10)